LONGMAN
EXAM
SKILLS

First Certificate
Reading

**Patrick McGavigan
and John Reeves**

Longman

CONTENTS MAP

Unusual hobbies

Developing reading skills

Lead-in

1a Match the names of the sports (1–4) with the pictures (a–d).

1 white water rafting

2 skydiving

3 bungee jumping

4 hang gliding

b Have you seen any people doing the sports in **a**, or have you taken part in any of them yourself? Where did you see them or take part in them?

2 Make statements about the people who do hang gliding, bungee jumping and skydiving, choosing the correct information from the table.

e.g. *Hang glider pilots jump from mountains or hills. They glide like birds.*

	Where do they jump from?	What do they do?
bungee jumpers	aeroplanes	glide like birds
skydivers	mountains or hills	jump using a special rope
hang glider pilots	bridges or high buildings	use a parachute to slow their fall
		perform movements in the air
		try to land smoothly

3 Look at the following newspaper headlines and match them to the sports in **1a**.

1 **Fatal fall as parachute fails to open**

2 **Young woman falls to her death from bridge**

3 **Heavy rains make river unsafe for sport**

4 **Lucky escape after bad take off**

5 Police stop office block being used for adventure sport

6 **Twenty-five link up in the sky over Birmingham**

Reading task: Multiple matching (headings)
Strategy: Looking for word groups

1a Skim (read quickly to get the general idea) through the following two paragraphs. You will see that there is a heading missing. (Do not focus on the words in *italics* at this stage.)

> ### The incredible world of scuba diving
>
> Scuba divers enter a silent and mysterious world every time they dive. They swim among hundreds of brightly-coloured fish, and larger fish move effortlessly past them. Dolphins sometimes approach them out of curiosity, sharks out of anger, perhaps, although they rarely attack divers. The strange underwater plants and the incredible colours of coral gardens are all part of the experience of scuba diving.
>
> | 1 |
> |---|
>
> The sport is not cheap, however. Divers must wear a proper *suit* which keeps them warm in cold water, while in tropical seas its purpose is to protect them against brushing against coral which can cut like hundreds of tiny knives, and jellyfish whose sting can be very painful or even cause the diver's death. A good quality *face mask* is essential, as is the *regulator* which supplies air to the diver's *mouthpiece* from the *tanks* he or she carries. There are also the *fins* worn on the feet and the *weight belt* used to help the diver descend.

b Look back at the paragraph under the missing heading 1 and at the headings **A–D** below. Match the word group in *italics* to the most suitable heading from the list.

   A The dangers of the sport
   B The diver's equipment
   C The undersea world
   D The importance of the diving suit

c Explain your choice of heading in **b** and say why you thought the other headings were not as suitable.

> **tip**
>
> Don't worry if there are some words that you don't know. Use the words that you recognise in the word groups to help you answer the question.

d Skim through the following paragraph from the same text on scuba diving. Choose the most suitable heading from the list **A–D** below, basing your answer on the main word group in the paragraph.

> | 2 |
> |---|
>
> In the past, the objective of many divers was to shoot specimen fish with spear guns. Now, though, instead of shooting fish, many divers would rather photograph them alive in their natural environment, and underwater photography has become a major feature of the sport. Feeding fish is something that many divers do as well. Indeed, in many places, the fish have learnt to associate divers with food and will come to feed as tamely from a diver as domestic pets take food from their owners. Wreck diving is another aspect of the sport that has always been very popular. Swimming through the cabins of a sunken ship is one of the strangest and most haunting experiences that scuba diving has to offer.

   A Changes in scuba diving
   B The excitement of diving
   C Diving activities
   D Different kinds of divers

2a Match the headings **(A–D)** to the correct word groups **(1–4)**. Try to do this exercise quickly.

   A Local entertainment
   B Essential camping equipment
   C A modern public transport system
   D Alternative energy sources

1

A warm sleeping bag, … a wind-resistant stove to cook on, … insect repellent, … a waterproof tent

2

Fast coaches, … a high speed intercity train link, … a monorail, … a clean and efficient bus service

3

Using the heat of the sun, … hydroelectric power, … wind-generated power

4

Two cinemas, … an excellent theatre, … several good-quality restaurants, … nightclubs

b You probably didn't know the meaning of all the words in **2a**, but could you still do the exercise?

Exam practice: Part 1

You are going to read an advertising leaflet about hot-air ballooning. Choose the most suitable heading from the list **A–I** for each part **(1–7)** of the text. There is one extra heading which you do not need to use. There is an example at the beginning **(0)**.

Key parts of the text are in *italics* to help you with some of the questions.

Remember!

Remember to look for word groups when matching the headings. You will also need to use other strategies.

A After your adventure

B Our flights

C Perfect for special occasions

D Make your dream come true

E Safety first

F Other services

G The right clothing

H What can you do on board?

I Where do we go?

---

exam tip

Remember that you are looking for the heading that matches best with the **whole** paragraph.

Champagne balloon flights

0   **D**

Bristol balloons invite you to fulfil the ambition of a lifetime. Experience a bird's-eye view of the countryside, while slowly drifting across the landscape, enjoying the magnificent sport of hot-air ballooning.

1

For a unique *birthday present, an anniversary gift or a celebration*, a flight in a balloon provides the perfect answer. You can even use our gift vouchers as an unusual and exciting present. Entertaining your clients or staff in a balloon provides something completely different.

2

Our aim is to give everyone a pleasant and enjoyable flight. Flights are available throughout the year and last for at least one hour. Allow four hours for the whole adventure. We lift off before sunset or soon after dawn because the winds are usually light at these times. We do not fly if it is raining or very windy.

3

Ballooning is the art of making pleasant and unexpected discoveries. We are *dependent on the wind*, so *no two flights are ever exactly the same*. The *average distance* we travel is ten miles, affording you views of the city and the surrounding scenery.

4

Many of our passengers are happy just to *relax and enjoy the view* and the incredible sense of peace that being aloft in a balloon provides. A balloon is a brilliant platform for photography. You might like to *bring a camera or a camcorder* and plenty of film!

5

For your safety and comfort we suggest you wear long trousers and long sleeves, and preferably natural fibres, like wool and cotton, which will keep you warmer than artificial ones. The weather can change very quickly, so even on a warm, sunny day bring a waterproof jacket. Something like a sailing jacket or a skiing jacket is ideal. Wear warm, waterproof footwear, and bring a hat if your hair is a bit thin on top. It will protect you from the heat from the burners.

6

Chilled champagne or orange juice is served with our compliments. Each passenger receives a commemorative flight certificate. Our ground crew who are in radio contact with the balloon meet us *on landing* and *will return you* to the departure point if required.

7

We have experience in operating advertising balloons in over fourteen different countries. If you have enjoyed your flight so much that you want to take up the sport yourself, *we can sell you* the latest equipment and *we can even train you* to fly your own balloon.

Language development

Word attack

1 Look back at the text on p.7. Find the words that mean the same as the following definitions.

    1 a strong desire to do something ....

    2 the only one of its kind ....

    3 an exciting journey or experience ....

    4 the last part of the day before it gets dark ....

    5 the time of day when light first appears ....

    6 things you find by chance ....

    7 the things you can see from a particular place ....

    8 does not allow water to go through ....

    9 the people who work on a ship, plane, etc. ....

    10 arriving on the ground ....

2 Complete the following sentences about mountain climbing, using the words from **Exercise 1**.

    1 We looked down at the wonderful .... from the top of the mountain.

    2 To get to the top of a mountain, climbers have to start every day at ....

    3 We climbed all day until ...., when we pitched our tents and got ready for the night.

    4 In 1998, a man with only one foot fulfilled his lifelong .... when he climbed to the top of Mount Everest.

    5 A climbing team made some very interesting .... They found flowers and plants that only live on that particular mountain.

    6 Climbers must wear warm, ... clothing.

    7 Climbing a mountain was a .... experience for me. It's something I will never forget.

    8 Climbing to the top of a high mountain was probably the most exciting .... I have ever had.

    9 The .... of the rescue helicopter risked their own lives to save the climbers.

    10 The rescue team had difficulty .... because of the terrible winds.

Showing what things are used for

1 Look at the example from the text on p.7.
*Something like a … **skiing jacket** is ideal.*

2 Match the words ending in *-ing* (1–6) with the nouns (a–f).

    1 sailing   **a** rod

    2 sleeping   **b** suit

    3 diving   **c** stove

    4 fishing   **d** rope

    5 climbing   **e** bag

    6 camping   **f** jacket

3 Complete the following newspaper headlines with the words from **Exercise 2**.

1
> **Successful underwater trial of new**
> ....

2
> **Frozen climber found dead in**
> ....

3
> **Tourist badly injured after explosion of**
> ....

4
> **Record fish landed by father on boy's** ....

5
> **Rough seas and icy winds prove effectiveness of new** ....

6
> **Man falls to his death after accident with** ....

Keep + noun + adjective

1 Look at the example from the text on p.7.

… wool and cotton, which **keep you warmer***…*

2 Complete the following text, using the correct form of *keep* and adjectives in the box.

| dry   quiet   safe   shut   tidy   warm |

Basic rules of good camping

Always (1) .... the campsite ....
Don't leave your clothes and equipment all over the place.

(2) .... yourself ....
When you leave the tent at night, put a pullover or jacket on.

Firewood and matches should (3) ....

(4) .... your tent door .... at night.
You don't want insects or snakes getting inside.

Make sure you (5) .... your valuables like money and
watches .... Don't leave them somewhere they can
be stolen.

Animals must (6) .... at night so they don't disturb
other campers.

Use of English

Read the text below. Use the word given in capitals at the end of each line to form a word that fits in the space in the same line. There is an example at the beginning **(0)**.

Adventure sports have increased greatly in **(0)** ....*popularity*........... over the last few	**POPULAR**
years. More and more people seem to be looking for **(1)** ...., perhaps	**EXCITE**
because they feel their lives are **(2)** .... Take, for example, the man who	**INTEREST**
sits in an office all day from Monday to Friday, but on Saturday he is an **(3)** ....,	**ADVENTURE**
risk-taking hero who participates in the most **(4)** .... of sports. He looks	**DANGER**
for the **(5)** .... cliff to jump from, strapped in a hang glider harness, or	**HIGH**
he is one of a crew **(6)** .... down a river moving at	**RACE**
(7) .... speeds. He is not difficult to recognise because he is the one	**TERRIFY**
who is often heard **(8)** .... about what he has been doing at the weekend.	**TALK**
He is always looking for an unsuspecting **(9)** .... to tell his stories to,	**STRANGE**
and he is always looking for the next thing he can do, which he thinks people will be	
(10) .... by.	**IMPRESS**

Competitive sports

Developing reading skills

Lead-in

1 Match the names of the sports equipment in the box with the pictures.

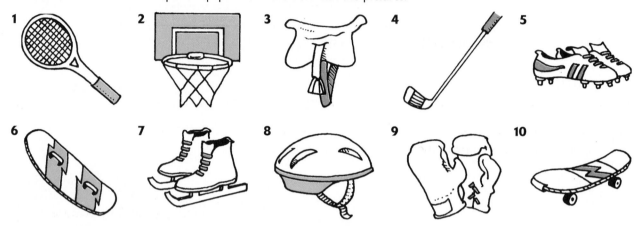

1   2   3   4   5

6   7   8   9   10

| basket   boxing gloves   crash helmet   football boots   golf club |
| ice skates   saddle   skateboard   snowboard   tennis racket |

2 Write the names of the sports in the box with the correct verb.

| basketball   football   gymnastics   handball   karate   motorcycle racing |
| skateboarding   snowboarding   tennis   weightlifting |

do: ....

play: ....

go: ....

3 Match what some sportspeople have said in interviews (1–3) with extracts from written articles about these same people (a–c).

1

A few years ago, I decided I was too old to compete any more, but I was really lucky because straightaway I was offered the job of coaching the national team.

a

Jill Green should have been an Olympic champion. She was three quarters of the way through the Marathon and well out in front when she broke down. She failed to finish. It was a personal tragedy for her.

2

It was the biggest disappointment of my life. With just five miles to go, I was leading the race. It was as if the gold was already mine, and then I got a terrible pain in my stomach, and I just couldn't finish the race.

b

Nick Davis retired from active competition in 1996 but he was immediately put in charge of the national programme, training the next generation of tennis stars.

3

I had lots of setbacks. The worst was when I got sick just before the biggest event in my career, but I didn't give up hope and I recovered in time to go out and win.

c

Kenny Maclish had lots of bad luck as a gymnast. He was struck by a terrible virus two weeks before the national finals, but he refused to be beaten by it and he got up from his sick bed to come out and take the title.

Reading task: Multiple choice

Strategy: Looking for words and phrases of similar meaning

1a Read the first two paragraphs of a text about a young swimmer.

> **Aiming for gold**
>
> Jamie is fourteen years old. He is a champion swimmer in his age group and his coach believes that one day he could win an Olympic medal. This is Jamie's dream.
>
> It's not going to be easy to make that dream come true, however, and Jamie already has a tough weekly routine. He puts in two solid hours of training before school and in the evenings, he is back in the pool or the weights room. Then there are the weekend sessions as well when he also has his homework to catch up on.

b Look back at the first paragraph and find a phrase that has a similar meaning to one of the multiple-choice answers below. Then choose the best answer (**A**, **B**, **C** or **D**).

1 Jamie has

A won a lot of swimming races.

B won competitions against people older than him.

C not taken part in competitions yet.

D won competitions against people the same age as him.

c Underline the key phrase in the first paragraph that showed you which answer was the best one.

> **tip**
>
> When looking for answers to multiple-choice questions, read the text carefully so that you don't miss key phrases that show you the correct answer.

d Look back at the second paragraph of the text and find a phrase that has a similar meaning to one of the multiple-choice answers below. Then choose the best answer (**A**, **B**, **C** or **D**).

2 Jamie

A is able to relax at the weekends.

B is very busy seven days a week.

C does swimming as his only form of training.

D gets less schoolwork than other boys of his age.

2 Read the rest of the text and underline phrases which have a similar meaning to the following sentences.

1 Jamie has to be able to swim fast and have the ability to keep going.

2 Successful athletes use their bodies and their minds.

3 An athlete's routine can be boring.

4 Olympic medal winners get plenty of money and they become famous.

> Jamie's coach explained that to do well at the top level in competitive swimming, he will have to have speed and stamina, and Jamie's training programme has been set up to develop these two qualities. However, that is not all, because to become a champion, you need not only to be in superb physical condition but you need to be mentally tough as well. That in itself is a justification for the demanding training schedule that Jamie already has to undergo.
>
> Jamie knows very well that he has years of constant training in front of him. His coach tries to make his training as varied as possible with several different kinds of exercises that they go through in the pool, but the unavoidable truth is that a certain amount of repetition and monotony is inevitable.
>
> On the other hand, Jamie is very aware that if he becomes an Olympic champion, his financial future will be assured and he will become a household name. Above all, he will have proved to himself that he is good enough to be the best in the sport that he has chosen to pursue.

Exam practice: Part 2

You are going to read a magazine article about a girl footballer. For Questions **1–7**, choose the answer (**A**, **B**, **C** or **D**) which you think fits best according to the text.

Key parts of the text are in *italics* to help you with some of the questions.

R e m e m b e r !

Remember to look for phrases in the text with similar meanings to the words used in the multiple-choice answers. You will also need to use other strategies.

I was about seven when I first started kicking a ball around with my brother. I was the only girl I knew who was keen on the game but I didn't care. Most of my friends were boys and *I enjoyed spending time with them* and that meant playing a game of football. It was my dad who noticed I had the skills to become a good player.

I loved football and it got on my nerves that I could only stand and watch when the boys were playing in real games in the local park. Whenever the ball came off the pitch, I'd kick it back in or do tricks with it. I just wanted to show them that I could do things with a football, too. Eventually, they got the message and I was thrilled when they gave me the chance to play. At last, I could play in a real team, but it did *seem funny that they were shocked that a girl could be a skilful player.*

In the competition matches, *no one expected to be competing with a girl and I had short hair so I looked like a boy.* We didn't hide anything from them and I never thought it would be a problem. As for the boys I played with, they just treated me like one of them. They didn't care if I was a girl, a boy or an alien as long as I kept scoring goals. Then one day, someone who was cheering me on shouted, 'Go, Kelly!'

After the match, the manager of the other team, who'd lost to us, came storming over to our manager. 'We're not going to play your team again unless you get rid of Kelly!' he shouted.

Then, in another game, when someone shouted, 'Go, Kelly!' again, one of the opposition supporters went to report it to their manager. For the rest of the game, I got lots of abuse from the players. *But the really horrible thing was when the parents started joining in.* I don't know what their problem was, but I can't help thinking it was because the fathers couldn't stand seeing their sons beaten by a girl.

It was hard not to let such hostility get to me but I made up my mind that I wouldn't let them see I was upset. 'Who are these people to stop me?' I said to myself, and I did manage to carry on playing through another seven games.

Meanwhile, word was getting around about the girl playing in one of the teams in our league. *More and more teams refused to play us* and eventually our manager decided he would have to have a word with my dad. The manager made it clear that if I didn't leave, the team would have to withdraw from the competition, so that was it. I had no choice but to leave.

After that, I gave up playing in boys' teams. I wondered if the standard would be as good in girls' teams, but the new all-girl team I joined was great. At first, I resented having to change teams like that, but after a while I really didn't miss the boys' league. I was still playing the game I loved and we won most of our matches that season.

Last year, our manager recommended me for a place in the England women's team, and I was selected! In my first match, I was the youngest player in the team and I was terrified when I first walked out. But hearing the crowd cheer and the national anthem, I was proud of how far I'd come. *I now know I would never have got so far if I'd stayed in the boys' league.*

I know plenty of people still see football as a boys' game, but my advice to them is go and watch some girls on the pitch. You will be surprised at the standard you see. *My advice to girls is,* 'Don't let what other people say put you off. Get involved in the game,' *and my advice to boys is,* 'Don't think you're the only ones who can play!'

1 Why did Kelly start playing football?

    A She liked being with boys.

    B Her father realised she was good.

    C Her brother played in the same team.

    D The boys saw she was skilful.

2 How did Kelly feel when the boys were surprised she could play well?

    A pleased

    B amused

    C annoyed

    D excited

3 At first, other teams

    A didn't mind playing against a girl.

    B objected to Kelly playing.

    C thought Kelly was a boy.

    D made Kelly feel uncomfortable.

4 What upset Kelly the most?

    A the behaviour of some supporters

    B the behaviour of her manager

    C the behaviour of players in her team

    D the behaviour of players in other teams

5 Kelly left the boys' team because

    A her manager thought she was a bad player.

    B she chose to give up football.

    C her father decided she ought to leave the team.

    D some teams didn't want to compete against her team.

6 How does Kelly now feel about leaving the boys' team?

    A She is glad she moved to another team.

    B She is angry that she had to leave.

    C She is sad that she was made to leave.

    D She thinks the girls' league is far easier.

7 Who was this article written for?

    A footballers

    B teenagers

    C parents

    D football supporters

Language development

Word attack

1 Look back at the text on p.12. Find the words and expressions that mean the same as the following definitions.

1 had a strong interest in ....

2 annoyed me ....

3 make somebody leave ....

4 didn't like something at all ....

5 became very determined to do something ....

6 have a short, private conversation with someone ....

7 expressed the facts strongly ....

8 make you not want to do something ....

2 Complete the following dialogues, using the words from **Exercise 1**.
Make any necessary changes.

1 A We've got a long-distance run in training today.

   B Oh, no! I .... those long runs.

2 A Can't we persuade you to stay with the club for another season?

   B No. I .... to move to a bigger club.

3 A What's the matter with the manager today?

   B The club .... to him that there's no money to buy new players with.

4 A I wish he wouldn't keep criticising other players all the time.

   B Yes, he's the only player in this team who ....

5 A Wouldn't you like to be a professional player?

   B Not really. All the training professionals have to do every day .... the idea.

6 A He's been saying to everyone that he's going to be the new team captain.

   B I know the manager .... this morning. He must have told him then.

7 A I'm sick of playing with her. She just doesn't try.

   B She's been told to try harder. Otherwise, the club .... her.

8 A You weren't always a footballer, were you?

   B No. When I was younger I .... basketball but then I got interested in football.

Win, beat, lose, miss

1 Look at the example from the text on p.12.

*I really didn't **miss** the boys' league. I was still playing the game I loved and we **won** most of our matches that season.*

2 Complete this local newspaper article, using the correct form of *win, beat, lose* or *miss*.

Weston take title

Weston United are the new champions. They (1) .... the league title yesterday when they (2) .... Bartford Town by 2 goals to 1. Highbridge Rovers (3) .... their chance to (4) .... Weston to the title when they (5) .... their last game of the season by 1 goal to 0. They obviously (6) .... their top striker, Danny Smith, who wasn't playing and his replacement, the 18-year-old Dean Jones (7) .... a penalty in the 89th minute. So Highbridge (8) .... even the 1 point they would have had from a draw in their last game and they finish the season in second place, just 1 point behind Weston.

At the other end of the table, poor Norton Rovers (9) .... by Eastwich in their last match of the season. This really came as no surprise to anyone because if they (10) .... yesterday, it would have been only their fourth victory of the whole season. This really has been a disastrous year for Norton.

Use of English

Read this extract from a leisure centre brochure and decide which answer **A**, **B**, **C** or **D** best fits each space.

The Burnham Leisure Centre has an impressive range of sports and fitness facilities which are all available to the public at a reasonable price.

Bring the family and enjoy the Olympic-size swimming pool or, if you're a serious athlete, you can **(1)** .... throughout the year on the all-weather running **(2)** .... You can even **(3)** .... snowboarding or skiing on the specially-constructed artificial ski slope.

If your game is tennis, you will find there are indoor and outdoor **(4)** .... to choose from. For team games, we have three five-a-side football **(5)** .... which you will probably have to book in advance because they tend to be very popular. Two basketball teams play at the centre, so you can always come along with the kids and **(6)** .... a match.

If you're just looking for the chance to get fit, why not take advantage of our superb **(7)** .... where you will find all the latest exercise equipment. We also run aerobics classes several times a week which provide low-stress **(8)** .... for people of all ages. After your workout, you can relax by taking a sauna.

1	**A** exercise	**B** practice	**C** train	**D** work
2	**A** ring	**B** track	**C** court	**D** pitch
3	**A** go	**B** play	**C** do	**D** make
4	**A** pitches	**B** fields	**C** rings	**D** courts
5	**A** pitches	**B** fields	**C** halls	**D** courts
6	**A** watch	**B** view	**C** attend	**D** see
7	**A** court	**B** gym	**C** hall	**D** room
8	**A** training	**B** running	**C** practice	**D** exercise

Computers

Developing reading skills

Lead-in

1 Label the computer system shown in the picture, using the words in the box.

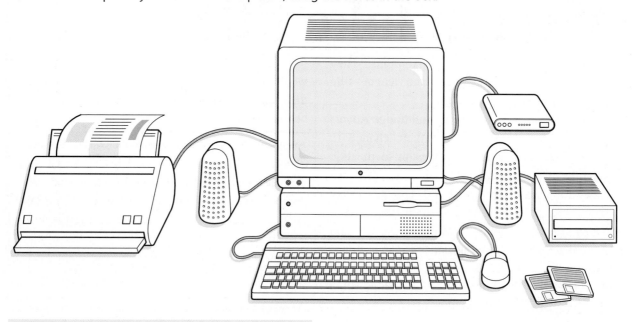

CD-drive   disk drive   floppy disks   keyboard
modem   monitor   mouse   printer   speakers

2 Make a list of people who use computers. What do they use them for?

3 Who might say the following?

1 'I love computers. In fact I have one at home and I use it to play games. The games are on floppy disks but the programs are on the hard drive.'

2 'I couldn't live without my laptop. I take it everywhere with me.'

3 'We upgraded our old computers by having CD-ROM drives installed.'

4 'Having databases of names and fingerprints is useful for us.'

5 'Our students can connect to the Internet to download software and also to find information for different research projects they are working on.'

Reading task: Gapped text

Strategy: Understanding reference words

1 Skim through the following text to get the general idea of the meaning. Do not worry about words you do not know. Choose a suitable title for the text. (Do not focus on the words in *italics* or on the gaps 1–3 at this stage.)

a The development of the computer

b The problems of having a computer

c Personal computer components

> **tip**
>
> Look for words like *it, him, her, this, that, them, they, such*, etc., which are small but important, to help in understanding a text. Try to work out what these words refer to in the sentences before or after them.

Although computers have been around for a long time, it wasn't until recent years that *they* became accessible to almost everyone. Approximately 60 million computers are sold each year. In the 19th century, Charles Babbage, an English mathematician worked out the principles of the modern computer. [1]

One of Babbage's designs had many features of a modern computer. *It* had an input screen and a store for saving data, together with a printer that made permanent records. Today, a typical computer has components to display and print information. *These* are the monitor and the printer. [2]

Nowadays, most computers come equipped with CD-ROM drives, which provide users with immediate access to a huge source of information; for *those* who want entertainment, the CD-ROM and the addition of speakers can bring a game or activity to life. With the development of the Internet and the World Wide Web, many computer-users now have access to an even bigger range of facilities, by linking up with other computers around the world. [3]

Another feature of high-technology machines is video conferencing. *Such* a facility enables people to see each other while they are talking on the phone through the Internet. If the people communicating through the Internet have mini-cameras connected to their computers, they can speak to each other face-to-face in real time. The need to be better informed is creating more powerful machines to provide society with all kinds of information and services.

2 Read the text again more slowly. Choose from the sentences **A–D** the one which best fits each gap (1–3) in the above text, using the reference words in **bold** to help you. There is one extra sentence which you do not need to use.

A **This** is achieved through a modem and a telephone line.

B Both of **these** involve training

C **It** also has a keyboard and a mouse to enter commands and data which is stored on and retrieved from the hard drive or floppy disks.

D At **that** time, the technology to put the theory into practice did not exist.

3 Look at the words in *italics* in the above text and write the words or information they refer to.

1 *they* (line 1) refers to ....

2 *It* (line 5) refers to ....

3 *These* (line 7) refers to ....

4 *those* (line 10) refers to ....

5 *Such* (line 14) refers to ....

tip

The reference word (*it, her, this*, etc.) does not always refer to words or ideas in the sentence immediately before or after the gap. You might also need to look at earlier or later sentences.

4 Complete the following text with suitable reference words. Sometimes more than one answer is possible.

Despite the advantages of using computers, there are also drawbacks. First, (1) .... are generally expensive to buy, maintain and update. There are also fears that the use of computers in education reduces human interaction and (2) .... may cause developmental problems in some students. A further problem is the availability of software. Educational computer programs can be bought but (3) .... programs may not suit the needs of individual classes. Teachers can adapt (4) .... software to suit (5) .... needs in the classroom, but this is time-consuming and often complicated.

Exam practice: Part 3

You are going to read an article about the uses of computers. Eight sentences have been removed from the article. Choose from the sentences **A–I** the one which best fits each gap **(1–7)**. There is one extra sentence which you do not need to use. There is an example at the beginning **(0)**.

Key parts of the sentences are in *italics* to help you with some of the questions.

Remember!

Remember to look for words like *it, this, those, they, them, such*, etc., when choosing the correct sentence. You will also need to use other strategies.

The computer and its uses

Few industries have changed so much in such a short time as the computer industry, and the pace of change shows no sign of slowing. The computer now has a role in almost every aspect of modern life, and it has radically affected the way people work, play, study and organise their lives.

As we enter the 21st century, computers are influencing ways of teaching and learning, as access to computers in schools is becoming more widespread and varied. **0 | H** In a teaching mode, computers provide a wide variety of information and practice material. They can also play a testing role in a range of subjects including Maths, English and Modern Languages. The one-to-one interaction students have with the computer, along with the immediate response to their answers, help to promote independent learning.

1 In the fast-changing world of business, employees are being physically removed from the workplace and the proximity of their colleagues, while remaining virtually connected via telephone, and the Internet. Laptop computers enable business-people who travel to have access to important information at the touch of a key. **2**

Computers are used to solve time-consuming data-management problems, such as payroll calculations, keeping stock records, bank account transactions, airline reservations, and scientific and engineering computations. Computers are also important in the collection, organisation, storage, retrieval and interpretation of information. **3**

In the film industry, computers are used to create graphics for scenes which would have been inconceivable in the past. This technique was used for films like 'Jurassic Park' where the incredibly realistic scenes of dinosaurs were all computer-generated.

4 Additionally, computer technology enables the training of pilots in flight simulators. Not only do these create the illusion of flying but they are safer and cheaper than training staff in aeroplanes.

In the home, the computer has become a great source of entertainment with the introduction of interactive Virtual Reality programs which are available on CD-ROM or through the Internet. They enable people located in different places to come together and interact with one another in real time using speech, sound and 3-D animated graphics. **5**

Nowadays, computers come equipped not only with a mouse, but also a host of different devices. Such components are essential if you are to spend any time on-line, whether it is playing games or researching any number of topics on the Internet. **6** It is possible to explore sites on anything you are interested in, or even chat with celebrities, experts and others who share your interest. Keep up with the latest news, fashions and reports. Look up facts on everything from who invented the plane to where to go on holiday.

In the future, today's technology will probably become obsolete as machines become more powerful. **7** The development of smaller machines will mean that it will be possible to condense all the written knowledge in the world into devices the size of a child's notebook. All human knowledge will literally be at your fingertips.

A *Another* area where computers are used is in the military, especially in the development of weapons and surveillance equipment to use in satellites for spying.

B *Here* you can access all kinds of valuable information and the beauty of it is that you do not need to leave your house to find it.

C *Then*, there may well be a microchip in each telephone receiver with more computing power than the huge machines of today.

D In fact, *they* are essential tools in almost every field of work from constructing models of the universe to predicting tomorrow's weather reports.

E Outside the classroom, computers provide people with greater flexibility and freedom, and also allow them to organise their time in a more productive way.

F Programs like *these* can often be downloaded free from different sites.

G Connections through a modem allow *them* to transfer data anywhere in the world.

H *Their* use enables the learner to develop at his or her own pace and makes the whole learning process more flexible.

I Computers are machines which take over more mechanical aspects of our brain.

exam tip

Read the sentences before and after the gap carefully.

Language development

Word attack

1 The text on p.18 contains the noun phrase *the pace of change*. Complete the text with the nouns in the box to form appropriate noun phrases. There are two nouns that you do not need to use.

century   fame   key   life   information   nonsense   technology   time

With the development of (1) .... in recent years, the way of
(2) .... for a great number of people has changed beyond
recognition. Because of increased speed in the transfer of (3) ....,
news and ideas travel around the world in seconds. Whatever we want to know is
available at the touch of a (4) .... Not long after the turn of the
(5) ...., scientists expect us to have computers which are so small
and powerful that they will fit into our pockets. Because of this, some believe that
newspapers and books will become a waste of (6) ...., as we will
have all the information we need through our personal computers.

2 The text on p.18 contains the phrase *It is possible* … Complete the following sentences, using the phrases in the box.

It is a good idea   It wasn't until   It is necessary   It is unwise   It doesn't matter **It seems impossible   It is incredible   It is only a matter of time**

1 .... to imagine a world without computers.

2 .... to have a CD-ROM drive to make use of multimedia facilities.

3 .... the mid-1990s that the Internet became easily accessible to the general public.

4 .... how our lives have changed with the advent of the computer.

5 .... before every household has a computer.

6 .... to leave CDs and floppy disks in direct sunlight.

7 .... to read the instructions on computer hardware carefully.

8 .... how old you are, it's never too early or late to learn to use a computer.

Word-building: nouns

Complete the table with the noun form of the words in the box.

accessible   attach   decide   defend   discuss   equip   explode generous   imagine   invest   mature   participate   violent

conference	development	illusion	possibility	information

Use of English

1 Read the text below. Use the word given in capitals at the end of each line to form a word that fits in the space in the same line. There is an example at the beginning **(0)**.

The impact of technology

The 21st century will no doubt see a great **(0)** .... *advancement* .... in electronics and   ADVANCE

technology as the **(1)** .... of computers increases all around the world.   POPULAR

For some, this technology will mean an **(2)** .... of their privacy, but   INVADE

for others it will be welcomed. In business and education as well as the home, the idea

of sending your **(3)** .... through e-mail is surely an exciting idea.   CORRESPOND

The greatest **(4)** .... must be the fact that there is no need to waste   ATTRACT

time going out to buy stamps and posting the letter off to its destination. Of course,

as our **(5)** .... on the computer and technology grows, there is also   DEPEND

the problem of **(6)** .... Users are afraid that personal   SECURE

(7) .... such as bank account numbers will become accessible   INFORM

to people who may misuse it. To combat this problem, there must be greater

(8) .... between banks and on-line services.   COOPERATE

2 Read the following sentences and decide which answer **A**, **B**, **C** or **D** best fits each space.

1 Having a computer allows you to have all kinds of information at your ....

    A arm   **B** fingertips   **C** fingers   **D** hand

2 She is a specialist in the .... of Information Technology.

    A job   **B** subject   **C** topic   **D** field

3 The Internet allows users to download free ....

    A sites   **B** hardware   **C** viruses   **D** software

4 Video .... can only be done if you have a camera with your computer.

    A conversations   **B** conferencing   **C** discussions   **D** meetings

5 The bigger the memory on your hard disk, the more .... you can store.

    A details   **B** money   **C** data   **D** transactions

6 Most hard disks today have a .... capacity of 200 megabytes.

    A storing   **B** memory   **C** huge   **D** storage

7 When you connect to the Internet it is said that you are ....

    A on-line   **B** on   **C** in-line   **D** integrated

8 A computer should be seen as a .... we use to help us do our work.

    A disk   **B** mechanism   **C** tool   **D** source

9 You need to have a lot of .... available on your hard disk if you want to run multimedia programs.

    A memory   **B** room   **C** area   **D** bytes

10 Technology has indeed had a significant .... on our lives today.

    A change   **B** role   **C** effort   **D** effect

Health and stress

Developing reading skills

Lead-in

1 Look at the photos of people in stressful situations and answer the questions.

    1 What is happening in each picture?

    2 How do you think the people feel? Give reasons for your answers.

    3 Have you ever been in any of these situations? How did you feel?

2 What situations are most stressful for you? What do you do to reduce the effects of stress?

3 What would you do to treat the following illnesses or problems? Use the ideas in the box or your own ideas.

1 a toothache	**5** a sore throat	**9** sunburn
2 a broken arm	**6** a high temperature	**10** a cut
3 a cough	**7** a rash	**11** a wound
4 an infection	**8** pneumonia	**12** a sprained ankle

> **have it set in plaster   put a plaster on it   drink lots of liquids**
> **apply some skin cream   stay in bed for a week   call a doctor**
> **use some antiseptic lotion   tie it up with a tight bandage**
> **take a painkiller   take antibiotics**

4 Match the words (1–8) with the definitions (a–h).

    1 ward

    2 prescription

    3 surgeon

    4 operating theatre

    5 injection

    6 symptom

    7 allergy

    8 anaesthetist

a a piece of paper on which a doctor writes what medicine a person should have

b a large room in a hospital where people who need medical treatment stay

c a medical condition in which you become ill or you get a rash because you have eaten certain foods, touched certain things, etc.

d a doctor who performs operations in a hospital

e a physical condition that shows you have an illness

f the room in a hospital where surgery is carried out

g a doctor or nurse who has been trained to give drugs to make you sleep during an operation

h an act of giving a drug by using a special needle

Reading task: Multiple matching (questions)
Strategy: Recognising additional information through relative clauses

1 Match the sentence beginnings (1–10) with the endings (a–j). Use the words in *italics* to help you.

1 Dr Brown, not Dr Harley, is the dentist

2 I like my nurses, most of

3 I don't understand

4 That's the cream

5 This is the ward

6 She is the only medical student

7 They are new drugs

8 The season

9 The woman

10 The reason

a *whose* diagnosis of the patient's heart condition was correct.

b *which* my doctor prescribed for my rash.

c *why* I have to take all these pills.

d *that* smiled at me as she went by is a surgeon.

e *where* heart patients are treated.

f *when* I suffer most from allergies is spring.

g *who* has a surgery in the High Street.

h *whom* are kind and helpful.

i *whose* long-term effects are not yet known.

j *why* I went to the doctor was that I was suffering from sleeplessness.

2 Scan (read quickly to pick out particular information) through the following short texts. Which sentence or sentences in the texts give:

a definition? `2`

information about people? ☐ ☐ ☐ ☐

a reason? ☐

information about places? ☐

examples of things that affect health? ☐ ☐ ☐

suggestions for improving health? ☐ ☐

information about a period of time? ☐

Use the words in *italics* to help you to write the number which precedes the relevant sentence in the correct box. Some sentences can be used more than once.

Stress

(1) Stress is difficult to define, but the majority of us *who* live in today's urban areas know what it is like: (2) it is the feeling *that* you can no longer cope with the everyday business of living. Stress plays such a big role in so many of the illnesses of modern life that it makes sense to try and do something to reduce it. (3) To do this, first you have to work out what situations are stressful for you and then think of ways in *which* you can avoid them.

Diet and health

(4) Diet is one of the factors *which* plays a role in keeping us healthy, and this is why we should pay more attention to what we eat. (5) Those *who* are overweight are prone to high blood pressure and cholesterol levels, *which* can cause heart disease, so it is important to eat wisely. (6) Remember, a healthy diet *that* is low in saturated fats and sugar can be just as enjoyable as one *that* is based on junk food. (7) Statistics also show that nations *whose* diet includes large amounts of vegetables and fruit tend to live longer.

Exercise and health

(8) Middle age is *when* most of us tend to lead more sedentary lives, but physical activity is important if we want to keep healthy. (9) It improves circulation and burns calories, *which* helps us lose weight. So get some exercise at least three times a week. (10) You can go walking if you live in an area *where* there are parks, or join a gym *where* there are aerobics classes for the middle-aged. (11) Do consult a doctor *who* can advise you about what kind of exercise is best for you if you are over the age of forty and haven't exercised for a long time.

Exam practice: Part 4

You are going to read a magazine article about how different people handle stress. For Questions **1–14**, choose from the people **(A–E)**. Some of the people may be chosen more than once. When more than one answer is required, these may be given in any order. There is an example at the beginning **(0)**.

Key parts of the text are in *italics* to help you with some of the questions.

Remember!	

Remember to look for words and phrases which add information about a person, place or thing in the sentence. You will also need to use other strategies.

Which of the people

has friends who are about the same weight? | 0 | A

wishes they looked different? | 1

says a particular time in their life affected their future? | 2

finds that being organised helps them to cope with stress? | 3

uses their imagination to help them calm down? | 4

believes that in the future they will benefit from going to a particular place? | 5

feels that very few people understand their problems? | 6

appears to have a new ambition? | 7

says that they are different from other people with a similar problem? | 8

was not especially clever at school? | 9

feels that their family contributes to their stress? | 10 | 11

benefits from something which is physically tiring? | 12 | 13

has both family and professional responsibilities? | 14

How I combat stress

A Kylie

Like every 15-year-old, I often feel under pressure about all sorts of things. I tend to be dissatisfied with my weight when I compare myself with girls *who* are taller and slimmer than me, but my mum points out that I am no different from the majority of my friends, *who* are really just as plump as I am. Another problem is schoolwork, and the end of term is a time *when* I get especially anxious because of exams. I have developed a range of strategies for periods when I have a lot to do and get really worked up. One of them is making a list of all the things *that* I have to get done, in order of importance. That way, I can plan my time better.

B Mario

I recently realised that my stress and anxiety is due to the absence of direction in my life. For me, schooldays were a time *when* I misbehaved and fooled about. I wasn't the brightest pupil around and I found most lessons very demanding. Sport was the only thing I was good at. This means that I now do not have the qualifications *that* I need to get a good job. So I have decided to set myself some goals and enrol at a college *where* I will be attending evening courses for adults next term. I hope this will give me the confidence *that* I lack, and better job prospects.

C Lukas

Being 16, my biggest cause of anxiety and stress is my future. I sometimes feel I shall never satisfy my parents, *whose* own professional success means that they expect me to do well in life. The only person *who* really understands me is my brother, and when we are together, we joke and talk about anything *that* makes us forget about our responsibilities. I have also joined a sports club, where I work out twice a week, and that has made a difference. After I have been to the gym, I find I am physically tired, but I have the mental energy to face the problems *that* seemed impossible to me earlier on.

D Nefeli

While I am aware that being overweight is a health risk, I don't get worried about my excess kilos or my appearance. Instead of just worrying about being fat, I go to keep fit classes, *which* is marvellous for reducing stress. Being active is not only good for losing weight but is also good for the circulation. I am not a fanatical weight-watcher, although I try to keep to a balanced diet *that* includes plenty of fruit, vegetables, whole grain bread and milk. I am not like those health freaks *who* tear around health food stores examining the labels on food products to see how many calories they contain. I just use my common sense. It amazes me more people do not adopt a similar attitude.

E Magdalena

I have a husband, four children, and a full-time job, which is a very good reason *why* I cannot call my time my own. There is always someone *who* wants something, or some job *that* needs doing. At the times *when* I can't cope any more, I sit or lie down and just close my eyes and think of somewhere quiet and relaxing – a warm, sandy beach, a grassy meadow or even the local park. Afterwards, I have a wonderful sense of relief and the things *that* I thought were urgent are not so important any more. Just a few minutes of this makes all the difference.

Language development

Word attack

1 The text on p.25 contains the phrase *under pressure*. Look at the phrases in the box.

> under pressure = having a lot of responsibilities
> under attack = being the victim of attack
> under development = something which is being developed or improved
> under the weather = feeling ill (idiom)
> under the impression = to have the idea or belief
> under control = being controlled or dealt with successfully

2 The verb *have* + noun is a very common pattern in English. Look at the examples in the box.

> **have a good time   have a rest   have a break
> have a headache   have time to   have a right to
> have no right to   have faith in**

Rewrite the second sentence in each pair so that it has a similar meaning to the first sentence. Use the appropriate phrases with *under* from **Exercise 1**, the appropriate phrases with *have* in the above box and the words given.

1 'I enjoyed learning first-aid at school,' Joanna told Vagelis.   HAD

Joanna told Vagelis she .... learning first-aid at school.

2 Unless you stop working for a while, you will feel tired.   BREAK

If you don't .... for a while, you will feel tired.

3 'You are not in a position to tell the patients what to do,' said the nurse.   RIGHT

'You .... to tell the patients what to do,' said the nurse.

4 'I am too busy to see you at the moment,' said the dentist.   NO

'I .... to see you at the moment,' said the dentist.

5 We had thought she was feeling well.   UNDER

We .... that she was feeling well.

6 He has a lot of responsibilities and strain in his work.   PRESSURE

He is .... in his work.

Word-building: negative prefixes

1 Complete the table by combining the negative prefixes *in-*, *un-*, *dis-* and *mis-* with the words in the box.

> **accurate   agree   allow   aware   direct   do   inform   known
> pleased   pronounce   understand   visible**

inability			
unhappy			
dislike			
mistake			

2 Complete the text, using the correct form of the word in brackets. Make all the words negative and make any other necessary changes.

He'll live till he dies

Not everyone cares about their health. Take my uncle Janek for example. He is the most (1) .... (health) person I know. We have tried to (2) .... (courage) him from smoking and sitting in front of the television all day, but he won't listen. Once he tried to get fit by jogging but he had an (3) .... (fortune) accident and broke his leg. After this, he was (4) .... (able) to get up from the sofa for weeks. Of course, he wasn't too disappointed about this but his wife was very (5) .... (happy) as she had to put up with him at home all day. She says lying at home doing nothing is a (6) .... (grace) and that he is setting a bad example to his children. His wife believes he is (7) .... (capable) of doing anything right and the way he lives is (8) .... (satisfy), but he says there's nothing to worry about, as 'he'll live till he dies'.

Use of English

Read the text below and decide which answer **A**, **B**, **C** or **D** best fits each space.

Clean living – it's enough to make you ill

In Britain, it is believed that asthma, which has doubled in children in the last 25 years, is due to air pollution. Certainly, the **(1)** .... of wheezing and shortness of breath can be made worse by exposure to traffic fumes, however, the risk of **(2)** .... asthma in the first place is highest in the least polluted parts of the country. Seeing air pollution as a **(3)** .... of asthma would seem to be common sense, but in fact, there is no relationship between the two. In our modern **(4)** .... world, we, and particularly children, are no longer exposed to the **(5)** .... that helped build the immune system in previous generations.

As with asthma, there are two other **(6)** .... conditions – eczema and hay fever – that are twice as common as they were 25 years ago. The three conditions run in families and tend to be '**(7)** .... of the advantaged'. In other words, they occur more frequently in children born in professional households and are more likely in small rather than large families, where there tend to be fewer germs being passed from one sibling to another. The rise in these conditions since the war years coincides exactly with the sharp decline in major childhood **(8)** ...., like polio, diphtheria, whooping cough and measles. They are thus presumably the 'price' that has to be paid for modern medicines and better social conditions.

1	**A** causes	**B** factors	**C** symptoms	**D** problems
2	**A** contacting	**B** taking	**C** making	**D** getting
3	**A** reason	**B** part	**C** kind	**D** cause
4	**A** hygienic	**B** curable	**C** immune	**D** natural
5	**A** allergies	**B** bacteria	**C** sicknesses	**D** antibodies
6	**A** allergic	**B** sneezing	**C** sick	**D** physical
7	**A** wounds	**B** injuries	**C** ailments	**D** cures
8	**A** rashes	**B** diseases	**C** reactions	**D** ills

Revision (Units 1–4)

1a Complete the table with the correct words from the box. Some words can fit in more than one category.

> boots   champion   court   e-mail   glide   hang glider   hardware   helmet
> land   monitor   multimedia   on-line   opponent   pitch   racket   risk   score
> sleeping bag   software   speakers   tent

Adventure sports and outdoor activities	Ball games	Computing

b Complete the following short texts with the words from **a**. Make any necessary changes.

1 That evening, I was lying awake in my (1) .... inside the tiny
(2) .... that I was sharing with two companions, thinking about the next
day. I knew it was going to be a day full of danger, but anyone who takes part in our
sport accepts its many (3) .... The three of us would spend the morning
struggling up the side of a mountain, carrying our (4) .... on our backs.
Once we were high enough, we would put on the (5) .... that we
always wear to protect our heads, and jump. If we were lucky, we might be able to
(6) .... for up to an hour and then find somewhere flat where we could
(7) .... safely. If we were unlucky, on the other hand, …

2 Both our children are sport mad. Susan, is a very keen tennis player. In fact, she
spends every free moment she has on the tennis (1) .... We recently
bought her a new (2) .... which, she says, has greatly improved her shots.
She is already the local under-sixteen (3) .... and she has beaten several
(4) .... who were older than her. Our son, Philip, has been crazy about
football ever since we bought him his first pair of (5) .... when he was
six. He plays in matches every weekend and on weekdays he likes to go out and
kick a ball about with some friends on a nearby (6) .... Last year, he
(7) .... more goals than any other player in his team.

3 Parents become concerned when they see their sons and daughters spending a lot of
time staring at their computer (1) .... Instead of going out and
socialising, many teenagers now prefer to send and receive (2) ....
through the Internet. Many stay (3) .... for hours every day. The problem
is not limited to the Internet, however. Many families now have computers which
can run sophisticated (4) .... programs with spectacular graphics
and sound effects. It is not surprising that once the parents have provided the
(5) ...., including the computer itself, a CD-drive and (6) ....,
their children will insist on having the latest (7) ...., such as space travel
adventures, racing and sports games, and quizzes.

c Choose the best heading from the list (A–F) for each of the texts (1–3) in **b**.

A An unpleasant sport   **D** A brother and sister team

B It can take them over   **E** Talented children

C An anxious night   **F** An educational pastime

2 Read the text below. Use the word given in capitals at the end of each line to form a word that fits in the space in the same line. There is an example at the beginning **(0)**.

You come across plenty of people who say they **(0)** ....*dislike*........ computers.   LIKE

These 'computer-phobes' resent what they see as the **(1)** .... of   INVADE

our lives by computer technology, which, they say, is used for **(2)** ....   STORE

information about people's private lives. Most are **(3)** .... of the   AWARE

many benefits computers can bring to users, like word **(4)** ....   PROCESS

which allows so many tasks to be done much more **(5)** .... than   QUICK

was possible in the past. They allow their fear to **(6)** .... them from   COURAGE

ever finding out about the extraordinary **(7)** .... of programmes that   VARIOUS

are now available, most of which are **(8)** .... easy to operate.   REMARKABLE

PC-users now perform tasks that would have been beyond the **(9)** ....   IMAGINE

of computer enthusiasts just a decade ago; that surely explains why there has been

an **(10)** .... of interest in computing all over the world.   EXPLODE

3 Read the text below and decide which answer **A**, **B**, **C** or **D** best fits each space.

For professional players like me, pressure is part of our **(1)** .... of life. We have to
find ways to **(2)** .... with the stress of big matches. Anyone who can't do this
quickly gets **(3)** .... the other players' nerves and then the whole team plays badly.
A player who can't stay calm can easily get himself **(4)** .... as well, or make stupid
mistakes. I remember a young player who panicked and gave away a penalty in the
first minute of a match. Luckily for us, the other team **(5)** .... it. He still couldn't
calm **(6)** .... after that and a few minutes later, he got himself sent off. With only
ten players, we were **(7)** .... attack for the rest of the game. In spite of this, we
managed to stop the other team scoring and in the second half, we scored the only
goal and **(8)** .... the match. You should have seen the look on the other team's
faces. They couldn't believe they'd been **(9)** .... by a team of only ten. As for our
young player, I am afraid it wasn't long before our manager **(10)** .... rid of him.

A lot of players I know relax by **(11)** .... golf. Some of them are so **(12)** .... on
the sport that they can't wait to finish their football training to rush off to the golf
(13) .... Personally, I can't **(14)** .... golf. I find it too slow, but what I do like
to do is to **(15)** .... bowling several times a week.

1	**A** type	**B** kind	**C** way	**D** method
2	**A** manage	**B** cope	**C** combat	**D** relieve
3	**A** on	**B** to	**C** at	**D** with
4	**A** damaged	**B** wounded	**C** injured	**D** bruised
5	**A** lost	**B** put	**C** scored	**D** missed
6	**A** down	**B** up	**C** out	**D** off
7	**A** with	**B** under	**C** at	**D** on
8	**A** beat	**B** won	**C** took	**D** lost
9	**A** won	**B** lost	**C** beaten	**D** beat
10	**A** had	**B** got	**C** made	**D** did
11	**A** doing	**B** going	**C** playing	**D** taking
12	**A** keen	**B** mad	**C** fanatic	**D** enthusiastic
13	**A** court	**B** track	**C** pitch	**D** course
14	**A** like	**B** stand	**C** learn	**D** accept
15	**A** play	**B** have	**C** go	**D** do

Shopping

Developing reading skills

Lead-in

1a Label the scene in the hypermarket, using the words in the box.

| cashier | credit card | customer | queue | receipt | trolley | till |

b What can you tell about the woman in the picture in **a**? Do you think she is single or married? What does she like doing? What is her home life like? Talk about the woman, using the following expressions:

I suppose she …

She probably …

She must …

2 Use the phrases (a–g) to say what happens in each of the situations (1–7).

1 You take faulty goods back to the shop.

2 You pay for your shopping in cash with a large note.

3 You go on a shopping trip with some friends.

4 You buy a new pair of trousers.

5 You don't have enough money to pay for something in full.

6 You buy a big amount of the same product.

7 You choose a new radio or a walkman.

a try it out in the shop

b get a discount

c hunt for bargains

d put down a deposit

e ask for a refund

f wait for your change

g try them on to see if they fit

3 Match the beginnings of the advertisements (1–5) with the correct endings (a–e).

1 Special discounts for

2 Great bargains

3 Full refunds are given

4 All methods of payment are accepted

5 Free service back-up

a within our twelve-month guarantee period

b including credit cards and cheques

c customers paying in cash

d if you're not satisfied with the goods

e in our winter sales

Reading task: Multiple matching (headings)

Strategy: Looking for word groups and examples

1a Skim through the following two paragraphs. You will see that there is a heading missing.

> **Present-day shopping**
> Over the last few years, shopping has undergone a revolution. Out-of-town stores like the huge discount stores and hypermarkets have been taking trade away from the traditional High Streets.
>
> | 1 |
>
> As the supermarkets have been moving out of the High Streets, interesting new shops have been opening up. The variety of little shops you can come across nowadays in a High Street is remarkable. There are expensive shops like antique shops and shops selling all kinds of hand-made articles. There are also pet shops, model-making shops, photography shops and the inevitable computer shops as well as bookshops, some of which offer a great selection of second-hand books.

b Look back at the paragraph under the missing heading 1 and at the headings **A–D** below. Decide which of the headings best corresponds to the word group and examples of shops given in the paragraph.

  A Shops offering good prices

  B Traditional shops

  C Specialist shops

  D Shops for unusual customers

c Explain your choice of heading in **b**, and say why you thought the other headings were not as suitable.

d Skim through the following paragraph from the same text on present-day shopping. Choose the most suitable heading from the list **A–D**, basing your answer on the word group and examples of shops given in the paragraph.

> | 2 |
>
> It would be wrong to suggest that the large stores have had it all their own way. Queuing for bread in a supermarket is not the same as visiting your local baker for freshly-baked bread and cakes. Many people still like to shop at their local butcher's where they can choose their meat carefully and tell the butcher how to cut it. Many greengrocers still do a good trade, too. Their customers enjoy chatting with them as they weigh and wrap their fruit and vegetables.

  A Traditional shops

  B Shops for old-fashioned people

  C The disadvantages of large stores

  D Special local shops

2 Write the correct heading **(A–D)** above the correct paragraph (1–4). Try to do this exercise quickly.

  A Convenience shopping

  B Shopping from home

  C Expensive shops

  D Outdoor shopping

> | 1 |
>
> Street markets are making a comeback in some places. People are rediscovering the pleasure of strolling through a market and browsing through what the various stalls have on offer. Car boot sales are an increasingly common feature of small town life. There couldn't be a simpler form of trade. People bring their cars to an empty field, open up their boots, and offer an often surprising variety of things for sale.
>
> | 2 |
>
> For many years now, mail-order shopping has served the needs of a certain kind of customer. Everything they order from a catalogue is delivered to their door. Now, though, e-mail shopping on the Internet has opened up even more opportunities for this kind of shopping.
>
> | 3 |
>
> Out-of-town supermarkets and hypermarkets are ideal for many modern families. There is always plenty of parking space around these shops and all the shopping can be wheeled in a trolley right up to the car and loaded straight into the boot. The best thing about them is that there is no need to visit more than one shop. Everything the family wants can be found under one roof.
>
> | 4 |
>
> Finally, there are the shops that sell exclusive products. These are the shops that, for example, sell furniture made by firms with reputations for the highest level of workmanship. There are also shops selling clothing and accessories which only stock famous brand names like Armani and Gucci. Then there are specialists in such things as hand-painted china, silverware and glass.

Exam practice: Part 1

You are going to read a text about shopping malls. Choose the most suitable heading from the list **A–I** for each part **(1–7)** of the text. There is one extra heading which you do not need to use. There is an example at the beginning **(0)**.

Remember!

Remember to look for word groups and examples in the text that match with the headings. You will also need to use other strategies.

A	Good family places
B	A choice of shopping
C	They will soon be everywhere
D	It's all so easy
E	Relaxing from shopping
F	A controlled environment
G	Escaping from the real world
H	Essential services
I	Not just a one-day experience

exam tip

Don't choose a heading just because it contains the same word(s) that you find in a paragraph.

Shopping malls

0	C

Originally an American concept, shopping malls, with their combination of entertainment and shopping, have proven to be irresistible to European consumers, who are as eager to spend their cash in them as their American cousins are. With malls now springing up in various parts of south-east Asia and in other areas of the world as well, it is hard to imagine that anything can stop them from spreading to all parts of the globe before long.

1

From the moment shoppers step out of their cars or off the bus that has brought them to the mall, they are encouraged to feel relaxed. Soft piped music is everywhere, in some cases even in the car parks. Security cameras monitor every inch of the mall. Many malls employ a small army of security staff to guarantee their customers' safety. And everything seems so clean, including the air within the giant buildings which is continuously renewed by tireless air-conditioning systems. Some malls permit smoking but only in specially-designated areas.

2

One of the basic reasons for the popularity of malls is the enormous variety of shops that are all to be found under one vast roof. There are sure to be several major department stores, not to mention supermarkets, all an air-conditioned stroll away from each other. An equally important part of the mall experience are the smaller shops and boutiques whose inviting displays make window-shopping a pleasure. Go inside, and you can browse through books, listen to CDs, purchase hand-made ornaments, expensive china, designer clothes, casual wear. The list goes on and on.

3

Non-stop shopping can be tiring, but there are a lot of other things to do in malls as well. Many people come to eat and drink as much as to shop. Malls offer a choice of places for people to sit, drink, and chat with their fellow shoppers, such as coffee bars, wine bars and, in the UK, traditional English pubs. There is always a good choice of places to eat, too, from American-style fast food outlets and steak bars to Indonesian or Thai restaurants.

4

It is a fact of life that children hate being dragged round shops, and here surely is another reason for the increasing popularity of malls. Their designers make sure that children are certainly not forgotten. Adventure rides, water parks, animal exhibits, historical displays and live performances by clowns are just a sample of the entertainment provided by malls to enable parents to take time out from shopping with their children when the kids have had enough.

5

Some of the larger malls even have hotels in them. Mall fanatics book in to give themselves enough time to have the complete mall experience. It is not only the restaurants and bars that are there to make an evening go with a swing, but there are cinema complexes and even nightclubs too in some malls, all within easy walking distance of each other.

6

Of course, these synthetic paradises exist for one basic reason: to part the consumer from his or her hard-earned money, so it's not surprising that all malls contain banks. Shoppers may need some extra cash for a few items that they had come to the mall with no intention of buying, or they might run out of small change for the entertainment on offer. For larger purchases, most credit cards are readily accepted inside the mall. Some malls have post offices and even sell postcards featuring the mall. There are first-aid stations as well in many of them which are clearly marked, just to complete the feeling of being in a completely safe environment where no one can come to any harm.

7

The mall is a wonderful fantasy land for adults and children. It's somewhere we can go if we want to get away from a miserable, wet winter or the uncomfortable heat of some parts of the world. It also provides us with a marvellous sense of security in a world that we have come to think of as more and more dangerous. Above all, it is a place created for the self-indulgent consumer, to serve his or her every need.

Language development

Word attack

Complete the following text, using words and phrases from the paragraphs under headings 0 and 2 in the text on p.33.

The first time I went to London was with some student friends. As students, we didn't have much money to spend and so we did a lot of (1) .... as we walked around the chic areas of London, gazing from outside the shops at the beautiful displays of elegant (2) ...., which we would love to have tried on. We also went round some world-famous (3) .... in one of which, as we were told, you could get practically anything you wanted if you had the money. We did find some interesting garments that we could afford in the little (4) .... we went into that specialised in cheap clothing for young people.

We also discovered that there is a great (5) .... of things you can do in the city that don't require a lot of money. A (6) .... through London's famous parks, for example, costs nothing and we went along to a music festival in one of the parks which was great (7) .... and was absolutely free. We sat there enjoying the music and spending what little (8) .... we had on ice creams and cold drinks.

Phrasal verbs

1 Put a tick (✓) next to each sentence which you think is correct. Put a cross (✗) next to any sentence you think is wrong.

1	Go and pick up a trolley.	**5**	He stepped off the bus.
2	Go and pick a trolley up.	**6**	He stepped the bus off.
3	Go and pick it up.	**7**	He stepped off it.
4	Go and pick up it.	**8**	He stepped it off.

> **add up   put down   save up for   shop around for   take back   try on   try out   write out**

2 Complete the following sentences, using the correct form of the phrasal verbs in the box. Make any necessary changes.

1 Before they go to the supermarket, many people .... a list.

2 It is a good idea to .... how much you spend each month so that you can keep a check on your finances.

3 If you don't have enough cash to buy something, you can often .... a deposit.

4 If you are not satisfied with something, you can .... to the shop.

5 It often pays to .... something you want. Don't just buy the first thing you see.

6 Before you buy an article of clothing like a jacket, ... first to see if it fits and if it looks good on you.

7 You can usually .... things like computer games and hi-fi systems in a store before you buy them.

8 If you don't have enough money to buy something that you really want, you have to ....

Compound adjectives

1 Look at the compound adjective from the **Lead-in, Exercise 3** on p.30.

... our **twelve-month** *guarantee period*

2 Write compound adjectives from the following phrases.

1 a coin worth two pounds ....

2 a note with the value of fifty pounds ....

3 a holiday that lasts ten days ....

4 a race of 400 metres ....

5 an exam which starts at 9.30 and finishes at 12.30 ....

6 a girl who was born in 1988 ....

3 Read the following advertisement about a house and some of its contents that are for sale. Then write six compound adjectives similar to those in **Exercise 2**, using the information about the house and its contents.

> The house itself has fifteen bedrooms and a lounge which is 20 metres long. The present owner had a golf course with nine holes built in the grounds. Of special interest in the contents of the house is a painting which is two hundred years old and a necklace which has been valued at around two hundred thousand pounds.
>
> A veteran Bentley sports car which has an engine with a massive capacity of six litres is also offered for sale.

Word-building: adjectives

Complete the table with adjectives formed from the words in the box.

> abuse act addition amaze appreciate delight disgrace embarrass emotion
> entertain exception explode forget pain peace politics protect thrill use worry

profession**al**	destruct**ive**	excit**ing**	wonder**ful**

Use of English

Read the text below. Use the word given in capitals at the end of each line to form a word that fits in the same line. There is an example at the beginning **(0)**.

A recent report has come up with some **(0)** ....*surprising*......... findings. It shows that SURPRISE
many people still prefer to do their shopping in **(1)** .... shops. They say TRADITION
they particularly like the **(2)** .... attention they get from local salespeople, PERSON
who take the trouble to get to know their customers and are always **(3)** .... CHEER
when they serve them. Many particularly like to buy **(4)** .... appliances ELECTRIC
from a local shop because they feel that if the products develop any **(5)** .... ANNOY
faults, they can take them back to a shopkeeper who they know and who they feel will be
(6) .... HELP

Another reason people give for preferring their local shops to the larger stores is that they
distrust the **(7)** .... salespeople they say they meet in the big stores. So it PERSUADE
seems that people are more **(8)** .... than we have been led to believe. The SELECT
report will make **(9)** .... reading to all of us who would hate to lose our COMFORT
local shops. It would indeed be **(10)** .... if they were to disappear. DEPRESS

Developing reading skills

Lead-in

1a Look at the young man in the picture. Complete the text about him, using the correct form of the verbs in the box.

afford   buy   pay   sign   win

He (1) .... the Lottery!

He (2) .... a large cheque

because he (3) .... a

beautiful sports car. He's so well off that he will be

able (4) .... for lots of

expensive holidays and (5) ....

to live in a luxurious flat.

b Look at this young man. Complete the text about him, using the correct form of the words in the box. Make any necessary changes.

bill   borrow   broke   coin   interest
lend   loan   note   owe

He's (1) ....! The only money he's got

is a handful of (2) .... and one or

two (3) ...., and he's got lots of

(4) .... to pay. He'll just have to ask a

bank for a (5) .... He'd like to avoid

(6) .... from a bank because he knows

they will charge (7) .... on any

money they (8) .... him. He'll end

up (9) .... lots of money to the bank.

2 Many countries in the world have a National Lottery. Does your country have one? If you won the Lottery, what would you do with the money?

3 Make sentences about a businessman's changing fortunes, choosing the correct information from the table.

e.g. *Alexander lost a lot of money when one of his ships sank.*

		a lot of money when one of his ships sank.
	earned	a small fortune in a casino when his luck was good.
	made	a high salary when he managed an investment bank.
Alexander	spent	a lot of money from his successful shipping company.
	lost	a fortune in a business that went bankrupt.
	won	a huge profit from buying and selling companies.
		large amounts of money on fast cars.

Reading task: Multiple choice

Strategy: Understanding implied meaning

1 Put a tick (✓) after the answers that you think are implied (suggested) by the following two statements.

1 Credit cards are wonderful if they are used sensibly.

A Some people are not sensible with credit cards.

B Some people are sensible with credit cards.

C Everyone uses their credit cards sensibly.

2 Action Oil's profits are disappointingly low this year.

A The company's profits are usually good.

B The company's profits were expected to be poor.

C The company's profits were expected to be good.

2a Read the first paragraph of a text about the fortunes of a man called James.

James' careers

James is one of those people who are good at lots of things, but somehow never quite manage to make a success of anything they do. He was good at his schoolwork and he used to tell everyone that he wanted to become a doctor. He didn't seem to be bothered by the thought of spending years studying in order to qualify. He talked happily about spending his life helping other people. Then, when he was in his last year at school, he was invited to play for an amateur football club which had a particularly good year in a local league. James became quite a star player, but that, I am afraid, meant the end of his future as a doctor.

b Look back at the first paragraph and look for the reason that is implied in the text to answer the following question. Choose the best answer (**A**, **B**, **C** or **D**).

1 James didn't become a doctor because

A he didn't want to spend years studying.

B he was good at football.

C he didn't prepare for his final exams at school.

D he didn't have the ability.

tip

Look for the **best** answer in multiple-choice questions. You will not always find three answers that are obviously wrong.

c Explain your choice of answer in **b** and say why you thought the other answers were not as suitable.

d Read the second paragraph of the text and answer the question that follows it. Choose the best answer (**A**, **B**, **C** or **D**).

James was a bit disappointed about not going into medicine, but he got over this quite quickly and decided to go into business. It wasn't long till he went into a partnership with a friend and they opened a shop selling sports clothes and equipment. The shop soon started to do well and James was talking confidently about opening more branches, and even suggesting that he and his friend would be millionaires by the time they were 30. Then a large store opened at the other end of town with a sportswear department. With a huge store to compete against, it was, unfortunately, only a matter of time before James and his partner were forced to close their shop down.

2 James was not successful with his own business because

A he didn't get on well with his partner.

B a big store opened next to his shop.

C his shop failed to attract customers.

D the big store's prices were better.

e Read the third paragraph of the text and answer the question that follows it. Choose the best answer (**A**, **B**, **C** or **D**).

That disaster left James with debts he had somehow to find a way of repaying. Since he was in debt, it would have been virtually impossible for him to open another business, so he had to find another way of making money. It was not long before he went abroad to work. He told us that he was going because he wanted to see the world. The last I heard of him, he was in America. He was involved in another new business venture which he was telling everyone he met would make him rich. Some things never change.

3 The writer believes that James

A really wanted to see other countries.

B probably won't become rich.

C is going to become rich in America.

D didn't have to go abroad to work.

Exam practice: Part 2

You are going to read a magazine article about a young Lottery winner. For Questions **1–7**, choose the answer (**A**, **B**, **C** or **D**) which you think fits best according to the text.

Remember!

Remember to look for implied meaning when answering the multiple-choice questions. You will also need to use other strategies.

The best present I got on my 16th birthday was the chance to play the National Lottery. I was really jealous of my parents and my older friends who put a bet on every week, so when I became old enough, I couldn't wait to have a go. I picked a set of numbers and from then on I used the same ones every time I played.

My school exams finished on 13th June, so to celebrate, I put £3 on a Lottery ticket. That evening, just Mum and I were at home watching the numbers being drawn on TV. As the numbers were called, my heart started pounding as I matched them to my ticket. 'Mum, I've won the Lottery!' I shouted.

We were so shocked we couldn't speak! Dad came home from work and I made him check the numbers too, just to make sure we weren't going mad. But even after he'd checked them, I still wouldn't allow myself to believe it, until finally I nervously dialled the number on the back of my ticket.

'You'll be contacted tomorrow morning,' said a voice at the end of the phone. I felt frustrated that I couldn't find out straightaway, so I just went to bed and listened to some music to try to take my mind off it.

The next day, I woke up early and phoned again.

'Well, Mr Selby, at the moment it looks as if you've got a winning ticket. Go to your regional centre and they'll confirm it.'

But the next available appointment wasn't until Tuesday! That meant I had two whole days to get through before I could find out if I'd really won!

Finally, Tuesday came round and with my mother and father I went to the Lottery's London office. There we met Alison Knight who looks after the prize payouts and she checked my ticket for about *half an hour* until finally she came out with my cheque.

'Congratulations, Mark,' Alison said, 'You're the youngest Lottery winner we've ever had. Here's your cheque for £127,000.' I was so shocked, all I could do was let out a dazed, 'Thank you.'

The next day, a press meeting was held at my karate club in Surbiton. All the papers were there, a TV crew even came and interviewed me – but it happened so quickly, I didn't have the chance to get nervous. That was my 15 minutes of fame, I suppose!

Since winning the Lottery two months ago, my life hasn't really changed that much. I've been quite responsible so far – I've put most of my money in an investment account so I'm not tempted to throw it away, and the interest I earn should give me a good income. But I have treated myself to a £500 watch and a £200 Playstation. I bought Mum a new jeep and I wanted to buy our house, but my parents wouldn't let me. I also gave my grandparents some cash to get some work done on their house.

And I've got lots of plans – I'm looking forward to my 17th birthday, when I'm getting a course of driving lessons. The car I want to buy is a BMW Z3. I think they're about £20,000 and I've had my eye on one ever since I won the money. I'm also going on lots of holidays next year. I'm taking ten of my family to Las Vegas. It'll be one big shopping spree. I'm going to buy lots of smart Armani and Calvin Klein clothes. I'll be taking my friends out for a meal in a posh restaurant soon, too.

As for girls, well I suppose it'd be nice to meet a girl who's cool and into soul music and karate. In fact, there's a model who I'd love to hear about my winnings and let me woo her with a meal in a pizza place ...

Of course, life will be easier for me now, but I'm determined it won't change me. People who say money has ruined their lives are just stupid. If it makes them depressed, they should give it to a charity who would appreciate it. I'm starting college in September where I have decided I don't want anyone to know about my win. I'm going to keep it to myself because I want to be liked for myself, not my money.

I'm just the same as before. I decided a long time ago that I wanted to become an airline pilot and winning the Lottery isn't going to make me change my mind. But I still play the Lottery every week – in fact, I'm already predicting my next big win, in the not too distant future.

1 Why did Mark Selby start playing the Lottery?

    A He wanted to celebrate his birthday.

    B He had carefully chosen a set of numbers.

    C People around him were playing it.

    D He knew his family needed money.

2 Mark knew he had definitely won the Lottery when

    A he watched the numbers being drawn on TV.

    B his father checked the winning numbers.

    C he dialled the number on the back of his ticket.

    D he went to an office in London.

3 After he got his cheque, Mark

    A became a famous person.

    B appeared on television briefly.

    C spent a lot of money on his friends.

    D became very popular at school.

4 What has Mark done since winning his money?

    A He has helped his family.

    B He has wasted his money.

    C He has bought himself a new car.

    D He has bought the house where his family live.

5 Mark

    A has changed his plans for the future.

    B has got a new girlfriend.

    C has not changed his plans for the future.

    D has made new friends.

6 Which statement best sums up Mark's attitude to money?

    A If you have too much money, it can be a problem.

    B If you have money, you should spend it.

    C If you have money, you should look after it.

    D If you have money, you should give some to charity.

7 Mark seems to be a young man who is

    A rather serious.

    B a bit of a dreamer.

    C rather big-headed.

    D basically sensible.

Language development

Word attack

1 Look back at the text on p.38. Find the words and expressions that mean the same as the following definitions.

   1 to make myself stop thinking about ....

   2 to come to the end of a difficult period of time ....

   3 is responsible for dealing with ....

   4 to lose or waste something ....

   5 be excited about something that is going to happen ....

   6 have noticed something and want to buy it ....

   7 not tell anyone about something ....

   8 change your opinion or decision about ....

2 Complete the following sentences, using the words from **Exercise 1**.
Make any necessary changes.

   1 She is the right person to talk to. She .... customers' investment accounts in the bank.

   2 I'm starting my first job next month and I .... to earning my own money.

   3 She has decided to save the money for a new car. Nothing you say will make her
....

   4 He .... a new hi-fi system and he is trying to persuade his parents to get it for his birthday.

   5 When Maria was making a lot of money, she .... She should have been more careful with it because now she's got nothing.

   6 I discussed our financial problems with my friend, Monika. The great thing about her is that whatever you say to her, she always ....

   7 We decided to stop worrying about our problems with money. We went away on holiday to .... them.

   8 If we can just .... the next six months, I'm sure the business will start to do a lot better.

Verb patterns

1 Look at the examples from the text on p.38.
   *... and I **made** him **check** the numbers ...*
   *I still wouldn't **allow** myself **to believe** it ...*
   *... but my parents **wouldn't let** me.*

> **Verb patterns**
>
> *make* and *let* + infinitive without *to*
> *force, allow, permit* + infinitive with *to*

2 Complete the following sentences, using the correct form of the verbs in brackets.

1 A I'd like to withdraw £500 from my account, please.

B I'm sorry, madam, but you .... more than £200 on this account. (not allow, take out)

2 A Why did you pay in cash?

B I had no choice. They .... me ....
.... by cheque. (not let, pay)

3 A Why have you changed banks?

B Because in that bank they .... you ....
.... ages before they serve you. (make, wait)

4 A Why didn't you just pay the bank half the money you owed?

B Because I .... the whole amount. (force, pay off)

5 A Can I cash this cheque, please?

B I am sorry, sir. We .... cheques unless the customer has proper identification. (not permit, cash)

Some uses of *hold*

1 Look at the example from the text on p.38.

... ***a press meeting was held*** *at my karate club ...*

a meeting a position (usually an important job like a chairperson or a director) an opinion, a view	**hold**	your tongue (when you shouldn't speak) your breath (when you are waiting anxiously for something) your head high (when you are proud of your actions)

someone responsible for

2 Complete the text, using the correct form of *hold* and the appropriate expressions from the boxes.

Edward Jones (1) .... the
.... of president of the
company for eight years before the company lost
money. Many people (2) ....
Edward .... for the company's
loss. Some even (3) .... the
.... that the company should
have a new president. Others disagreed.

Finally, a (4) .... was
.... to decide whether Edward
should remain as the president. All the
important people in the company were present.
Edward believed he had done his job well and
he could (5) .... Still, he
was nervous and he (6) ....
when the decision about his future was
eventually taken. It was agreed that he could
continue as the company's president for a trial
period of twelve months.

Get something done

1 Look at the example from the text on p.38.

*I gave my grandparents some cash to **get some work done** on their house.*

2 Read the following text about why a man urgently needs £1,100. Write sentences about what he needs to get done.

e.g. *He needs £50 to get the television repaired.*

'Money! We need lots of it. There is so much that needs doing. The television has just broken and that'll be a repair bill of about £50, I'm sure. The paint is falling off the house in places. A painter who looked at it said it would be a £500 job. My car needs a service. The garage tell me that will cost about £300. On top of that, it's time to replace the tyres, so that will mean another £150. The cooker needs mending, too, and the service engineer who looked at it said it could cost up to £100.'

Work

Developing reading skills

Lead-in

Look at the following job advertisement and answer the questions.

MANAGER WANTED

Herbal Health, Madrid

Herbal Health is one of the world's leading companies in health and dietary products.

Applications are invited for the post of Manager at our Madrid store.

Applicants must speak English, be computer literate, have administrative experience and an interest in health and lifestyle issues. An ability to speak Spanish is an advantage, although language training will be provided.

Responsibilities include day-to-day running of the store together with recruitment and training of new staff. The manager acts as a representative for the company and is expected to provide excellent service to customers.

Contact Sue Jones on (00 44) 181 744 1243 for more information.

---

1 Do you think the above job would suit you? Why/Why not?

2 Tell your partner what skills or qualities you might need for this kind of job.

3 Which of the adjectives in the box would you associate with the jobs in the pictures below? Give reasons for your answers.

---

calm daring determined emotionally strong hardworking honest
methodical patient physically strong quick-thinking responsible sociable

Reading task: Gapped text

Strategy: Looking for associated words and ideas

1 Read the following text and choose the sentence below which best fits each gap (1–3), using the words in *italics* to help you. In the example (0), the words in *italics* are associated with the word in **bold**.

Careers

My association with wood started when my father let me play with some of his tools. I loved it so much that he began to show me *how to cut*, *saw* and *drill* bits of wood and create different shapes. **[0]** These were **skills** which improved with experience and time and soon I became very good at handling wood. My knowledge and ability developed, until at the age of 16, I decided to become a carpenter.

I was very lucky because my *choice of career* was clear. **[1]** There are many things to consider and many questions to ask about the right type of job, qualifications, skills and earnings. These are questions usually considered by dynamic and ambitious young people who want a position with a high salary and good *prospects for promotion*. **[2]**

Early school-leavers usually take poorly paid, low-skilled jobs with no real future. They do not realise that without *qualifications or skills* they will probably stay in the same job with the same status for most of their working lives. **[3]**

Equally important for a successful career are job skills which have been learned at the place of work. In recent research, it was shown that the ability to apply yourself to your work is the key to success in the world of industry and commerce, as jobs become more dependent on the flexibility, analysis and judgement of the employee.

1 **A** For most young people, however, deciding about their future is very difficult.

   B It's always very important to choose the right subjects.

   C I knew I had to get a good job.

2 **A** For those who lack skills and qualifications, opportunities for moving up the career ladder are rare.

   B Getting a high salary is important.

   C You need to think how you will behave when you are a manager.

3 **A** And so a university education is essential.

   B It is therefore important for young people to get as much education or vocational training as possible.

   C As a result, they will never get promoted.

2 Read the last paragraph again and underline the examples of associated words and ideas.

Exam practice: Part 3

You are going to read an article about a model called Bridget Hall. Seven sentences have been removed from the article. Choose from sentences **A–H** the one which fits each gap **(1–6)**. There is one extra sentence which you do not need to use. There is an example at the beginning **(0)**.

Remember!

Remember to look for associated words and ideas in the missing sentences which relate to the main text. You will also need to use other strategies.

The making of a model

Having been under her mother's wing for most of her life, Bridget Hall now makes her own career decisions as a model. Bridget made her first professional appearance at the age of nine. She hated her first assignment, which was during a heatwave, and for which she was paid a fee of $75 an hour. | 0 | **C**

Such a life takes its toll, however, as it demands a strong sense of commitment. Once contracts have been signed, Bridget's time is not her own as she has to be willing to work long hours on shoots in distant places. Additionally, she has to keep her body in tip-top physical condition through diet and exercise. | 1 |

Modelling is obviously a tough business which requires single-mindedness and determination to succeed. Bridget believes she has both but she is also thankful to her mother, Donna, for her encouragement. She says lovingly of her mother that she was very supportive in the early days when jobs were not always available and money was scarce. | 2 | The problem was that she became too tall to model with other children and subsequently was unemployable for some time.

When Donna, Bridget's mother, suggested a shift to modelling ladies' clothes, the agency was rather reluctant. Undaunted by this, Donna hired a make-up artist and hair stylist and then booked a session in a studio to get new photographs for a portfolio which was sent to all the big agencies. | 3 |
Bridget was an immediate hit.

Encouraged by Bridget's new-found success, a major agency got her to sign a two-year contract. Today Bridget earns a minimum of $10,000 a day. Despite her new wealth and status, she admits that she might have made some bad decisions when she was younger. | 4 |

Bridget is aware of the gaps in her education and the subject of completing her studies does come up in discussions from time to time, but until now, she has not felt strongly motivated to do anything about it. | 5 |

In fact, her talk of education stopped completely when she met actor Leonardo DiCaprio and they became good friends. Bridget is a very popular individual and the fact that she keeps company with such celebrities means that she is frequently invited to occasions of all sorts. At an all-star party in her honour in New York, 1500 turned up at a bar–restaurant to celebrate with her. | 6 |
All in all, the price of fame and stardom must be well worth paying.

A Given her fast and furious lifestyle, it is hardly surprising that Bridget has not gone back to the classroom.

B The time and investment were well spent, as the reaction to the new pictures was overwhelmingly enthusiastic.

C Her working conditions and income have changed since then, and she now chooses where and when to work, and loves the excitement and glamour of the fashion world.

D Like a true professional, Bridget goes jogging every day and restricts herself to high-protein, low-calorie meals.

E Bridget enjoys her hectic social life, although it can be very exhausting.

F She sometimes regrets that she dropped out of school so early but the attraction of high modelling fees helped to lure her away.

G Having spent most of her life as a model she has many regrets.

H Somewhere between Bridget's twelfth and thirteenth birthdays, her bookings began to drop off.

exam tip

Read the whole text first to get the general idea of what it is about. Then skim the missing sentences to find associated words and ideas.

Language development

Word attack

1 Look at the example from the text on p.44.

*... as it demands a **strong sense** of commitment.*

2 Complete the table, using the nouns from the box which collocate with the adjectives given.

> breath hopes relationship season sleep standard
> stomach terms thinker trouble winds words

strong	high	deep

3 Complete the following sentences, using the phrases from **Exercise 2**.

1 She had .... of getting promotion after three years of work.

2 To be a surgeon you need to have a .... to stand the sight of blood.

3 The manager was in .... with his boss for having forgotten to prepare the report.

4 The director told the staff in very .... that she would not allow smoking on office premises.

5 Our company has reached a .... of production which we wish to maintain.

6 Elena was in such a .... that her father couldn't wake her up for work.

7 My company thinks there's a .... between an employee's job satisfaction and their level of productivity.

8 The .... for the tourist industry is July and August.

Phrasal verbs and compound nouns with *work*

Phrasal verbs

to work out (a problem)

to work up (an appetite)

to work on (something)

to work off (stress)

Compound nouns

a workstation = the part of an office or factory where you work

a workout = a period of physical exercise

a workload = the amount of work a person or machine is expected to do

a workshop = a room or building where machines are used for making or repairing things

a workmate = someone you work with

Complete the following sentences, using the verbs and nouns from the box on p.46. Make any necessary changes.

1 She had a heavy .... and was exhausted each day.

2 When our machinery breaks down, we take it to our .... to be repaired.

3 Scientists are .... finding a solution to the problem of pollution.

4 Going to a gym for a .... is a great way to relax.

5 As I wasn't very hungry, I went for a run to ....

6 One of her .... does a lot of overtime just to earn extra money for her holidays.

7 His .... at the office is always very neat and tidy.

8 We couldn't .... what was wrong with the machine so we called for a technician.

Word-building: jobs

Complete the table with more examples of jobs with the same endings.

account**ant**	lawy**er**	dent**ist**	act**or**	magic**ian**

Vocabulary connected with work

1 Complete the following text, using the words in the box. Make any necessary changes.

> **apply   career   electrician   living   overtime   retirement   skilled   trade   unemployed   wages**

Christopher had left school at the age of sixteen and (1) .... for a job as an apprentice (2) .... He loved electrics and there was nothing he couldn't fix. His father had wanted him to study and have a (3) .... in business, but Christopher had decided he wanted to work in the building (4) .... His first (5) .... were £10 a week, which was not very much, but he was able to make more with some hours' (6) .... at the weekend. Christopher knew that when he became a (7) .... tradesman he would earn a good (8) .... Christopher has worked for several different firms and has been fortunate never to be (9) .... in his life. He loves his work, although he does look forward to his (10) .... when he can spend more time on his hobbies.

2 Complete the sentences, using the words in the box.

> **commitment   compassion   efficiency   experience   prospects   skills**

1 You need dedication and .... to get to the top of any field.

2 To be a politician, good public-speaking .... are required.

3 Punctuality and .... are important for work with the public.

4 You need to have a deep .... for animals to be a vet.

5 If you work at that firm, you will have good promotion .... for the future.

6 Qualifications and previous work .... are essential for this post.

Developing reading skills

Lead-in

1a Look at the pictures and use the words in the box below to describe the kinds of things you think you can do and see in each place.

1
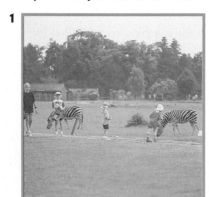

2

3

adventure rides   'learning by doing'   nature   parklands
picnic area   plants   refreshments   restaurant   roller coasters
roundabouts   swings   water slides   wildlife

b Match the following statements to the pictures in **Exercise 1**.

1 'Photographing wild animals up close was amazing!'
2 'It was a real hands-on learning experience.'
3 'I was scared stiff before I went on, but I really enjoyed it – when it was over!'
4 'It was lovely to eat outside in a beautiful setting.'
5 'We had the time of our lives on all the rides!'

2 Which of the places would you like to visit? Why?

Reading task: Multiple matching (questions)

Strategy: Looking for words and phrases of similar meaning

exam tip

Try to look for words and phrases in the texts that have a similar meaning to those in the questions, e.g. *I couldn't see* (in the question) = *it was hard to make out* (in one of the texts).

1 Scan through the three texts about different places (**A–C**) and decide which statement 1–8 corresponds to which text. Use the words in *italics* in the texts to help you.

At which place

could you come across things you don't often see?
 1

is travelling from place to place very easy?
 2

would it be cheaper for people if they came as a group?
 3

would you get to understand a place better?
4

do they change what is on according to the time of year? ☐ 5

could you buy things in shops with an international reputation? ☐ 7

do they provide visitors with a 'learning by doing' experience? ☐ 6

do they have the most up-to-date entertainment of its type? ☐ 8

A Bristol Zoo

Enjoy a day out with a difference. Experience over 300 amazing species of animals at close quarters in the Zoo's beautiful gardens. Enjoy *rare encounters* with real wildlife in a range of habitats. This fun-filled *interactive approach* is part and parcel of the most memorable family day out you could imagine. Now widely regarded as the best zoo in the country, we've earned that reputation by creating an animal- and child-friendly environment *where the accent is always on involvement*. Feast your eyes at feeding times and find out more fascinating facts from one of our informative Keeper Talks. Then feel what it is like to stroke a crocodile or leopard at one of our regular touch table teach-ins. At the aquarium, venture deep into the silent world of underwater creatures, or at Lake Island, *catch a glimpse* of the lively monkeys and lemurs among the trees, while ducks and pelicans nest among the reeds below.

A *special discounted rate is available to parties*.

B Alton Towers

Come to Alton Towers for thrills and spills beyond your wildest imagination. Alton Towers, Britain's number one theme park, offers you *state-of-the-art ride technology* with the world's first vertical drop roller coaster. Step aboard 'Oblivion' and prepare yourself for the most terrifying experience of your life! There's something for everyone at Alton Towers – from the thrill of the other big rides to the beautifully enchanting world of Beatrix Potter and the spectacular new Ice Show. Children are spoilt for choice with two specially themed areas just for younger visitors and over 25 rides and attractions for the under eights. And when hunger sets in, there's plenty of food with a wide choice for all tastes in on-site restaurants which have been recently revamped.

C Visitors' London

Getting around London *is a breeze* on one of the numerous coach tours. Coaches stop at all major attractions giving a full tour of the city. London is home to treasures of the world's civilisations but treasures of a different kind can also be found *in boutiques of world renown* catering for every taste, from clothes to souvenirs to diamonds and caviar. Another kind of shopping can be found at the restored Victorian market at Covent Garden with its diverse range of goods on stalls selling everything from inexpensive jewellery to second-hand books. This is truly a street market which *gives you an insight into* another way of life in London. With its *seasonal programme of events and activities* providing plenty of fun and entertainment throughout the year, Covent Garden is always alive. The highlight of each season's program is a colourful festival with spectacular firework displays lighting up the sky. Most restaurants feature a wide selection of dishes and light snacks.

2 Find the words and phrases in the texts which mean the same as the following definitions.

1 only a short distance away ....

2 included in ....

3 enjoy watching ....

4 the excitement and danger involved in an activity ....

5 having so many good things to select from that you can't decide what to do or have ....

6 begins to make itself felt ....

7 wide variety ....

8 providing people with all the different things they might like ....

Exam practice: Part 4

You are going to read some information about different places to visit in the West of England. For Questions **1–16**, choose from the places **(A–E)**. Some of the places may be chosen more than once. When more than one answer is required, these may be given in any order. There is an example at the beginning **(0)**.

Remember!

Remember to look for words and phrases in the texts which have a similar meaning to those in the questions. You will also need to use other strategies.

At which place(s) could you

travel by train from one place to another?		0 A
find out more about military history?		1
pay less by going with a group?		2
go on a mysterious journey?		3
see examples of farming equipment?		4
find facilities for eating outside?		5
see a material being made?		6
go for a gentle walk?	7	8
find equipment for physically-handicapped people?		9
see impressive buildings?	10	11
enjoy yourself if you are keen on horticulture?	12	13
benefit from arranging the visit beforehand?	14	15
order wine with a meal?		16

Visiting the West of England

A Longleat Park

Longleat is much more than a splendid stately home and exciting Safari Park. It has its own railway which takes you from site to site. There is the world's largest maze, where you can get lost for hours, or, why not visit the intriguing Adventure Castle? For those who are interested in animals, there is a safari by boat. All kinds of refreshments are available in the café, or if you prefer, there is a peaceful picnic area. The best way to take advantage of this unique and entertaining venue is on foot, so take it easy and wander around the grounds at will. Longleat House is open to the public every day from Easter to September from 10 a.m. till 6 p.m. The rest of the year the opening times are from 10 a.m. until 4 p.m.

B Worldlife

Take a break and enjoy the fascinating experience at Worldlife, amongst living butterflies and exotic plants. There are conservation displays, tropical birds and animals and a beautiful house and grounds which are rich in vegetation and flora. Facilities also include a play area with all kinds of rides and activities. Education and enjoyment go hand in hand so at the Lullingstone Silk Farm witness the unique rearing, reeling and production of English silk, as supplied to royalty. Open daily from 10 a.m. to 5 p.m. from April to September. Opening times may be subject to change. Coach parties are welcome if booked in advance.

C Crinkley Bottom

Bring the family to Britain's first TV leisure park and enjoy a wonderful land of make-believe. On hot sunny days, shoot the rapids on our sensational new water ride or take a stroll through the beautiful gardens and parkland at your leisure. Take a camera and get snapshots of some of the amazing wildlife roaming around the grounds. For those with a real sense of excitement, take a chance and join the adventure treks for a trip into the unknown. If it is entertainment and laughter you seek, then try the Fun Village. The venue provides fabulous family entertainment throughout the day with a varied and lively programme. Come and enjoy a host of events and have a wild day out!

D Abbotsbury

Open 7 days a week from 10 a.m. to 6 p.m. from Easter to October. In the swannery you can visit over 600 friendly, free-flying swans which are quite different from angry river swans. Enjoy the captivating experience of helping to feed the birds between 12 p.m. and 4 p.m. daily. Rare poultry can be fed by children. There is also a working dovecote with over 100 doves. Take pleasure in marvelling at the magnificent 18th-century walled garden with its rare and exotic plants. There is an adventure play area, a gift shop and tea garden. In the tithe barn, one of the oldest thatched barns in the world, there is a fascinating collection of rural tools, machinery and exhibits. A family super saver ticket with up to 30% discount is available. There are reductions for pre-arranged parties of 15 or more.

E Fleet Air Arm Museum

If it's excitement you are looking for, then visit the Fleet Air Arm Museum, Somerset, which is located in realistic settings and contains over 40 aircraft, including planes from World War I, and numerous photographs and film shows depicting the history of the Royal Navy Air Force. Take your time to explore the superb award-winning 'Ultimate Carrier Experience', a flight deck on land with all the sights, smells, sounds and actions of an aircraft carrier on a mission of mercy at sea. An interactive audio and visual show brings the place to life. Facilities include a licensed restaurant, free parking in the massive car park, a gift shop and a children's adventure playground. For disabled members of the public, there are special facilities. Additional facilities include a babycare centre with specially-trained staff who look after the children if they want to take a nap.

Language development

Word attack

1 Look at the example from the text on Longleat Park on p.51.

The best way to **take advantage** *of this …*

2 Find the phrases in the texts on p.51 starting with *take* which mean the same as the following definitions.

1 risk ....

2 not rush ....

3 have a leisurely walk ....

4 a short sleep ....

5 relax ....

6 have some time off ....

7 enjoy the fact ....

8 make good use ....

3 Complete the following text, using the correct form of the phrases with *take* from **Exercise 2**. Two of the phrases are not necessary.

On your next day off, why don't you
(1) .... of our special family saver tickets? Come to Euro-Leisure for the experience of a lifetime! What better way to relax than to (2) .... around the grounds of our wonderful site. There's no need to hurry, just
(3) .... to enjoy all the sights and soak up the magic of the venue. We (4) .... in knowing that we have award-winning displays and attractions and that we know how to present them to the public. You deserve it to
(5) .... and get away for the day. We have such wonderful covered facilities that you don't ever need
(6) .... with the weather, so if it rains, you can still enjoy yourself.

Phrasal verbs

1 Look at the example from the text on The Fleet Air Arm Museum on p.51.

If it's excitement you are **looking for**, *…*

2 Complete the sentences, using the correct form of *look* and the words in the box.

> **back   back on   down on   for**
> **forward to   into   out for   up**

1 The children were very disappointed not to be able to go to the theme park, as they .... it for weeks.

2 At 'Yesterday's World', we had the opportunity .... and see how people lived in the past.

3 See life as experienced by people a hundred years ago and witness how members of the aristocracy .... the poor and uneducated.

4 At 'Future World', you can .... the future and find examples of technology that will be used.

5 If you are .... a free day out, there are plenty of parks and museums to visit.

6 While you are wandering around the site, ... the Water exhibit.

7 Take lots of snapshots and have something of your visit to ....

8 Find out all you want to know about the site by .... it .... in our guidebook.

Use of English

1 Read the text below and decide which answer **A**, **B**, **C** or **D** best fits each space.

Drayton Manor Park

What makes a visit to Drayton Manor the best-value family day out in Britain? The park **(1)** .... in over 250 acres of magnificent parkland, and you'll find an amazing thrill-a-minute theme park with more exciting rides than you could possibly imagine. It **(2)** .... for everyone from children to grandparents. There is a fabulous 15-acre zoo, a fun-packed Children's Corner, life-size dinosaurs, **(3)** .... entertainment and snack stops. In fact, **(4)** .... enjoyment where the whole family can **(5)** .... fun at affordable prices. Drayton Manor **(6)** .... a spectacular zoo filled with animals of all shapes and sizes. Also in the **(7)** .... , there is Europe's only stand-up roller coaster with its 40-metre drop, and the make-believe world of Cowboy Town, where you can **(8)** .... the Rio Grande Railway or colourful horses.

(9) .... are available throughout the park at different locations for when you need a snack. Groups are welcome and there is a fixed **(10)** .... price for parties of more than 27. Unlike other theme parks, prices are not **(11)** .... to change, although the management reserves the right to close rides for technical reasons. This exciting **(12)** .... is open from March to November each year.

1	**A** locates	**B** is parked	**C** stands	**D** is lying
2	**A** suggests	**B** offers	**C** caters	**D** looks
3	**A** live	**B** living	**C** life	**D** alive
4	**A** fast-stop	**B** never-stopping	**C** non-stop	**D** unstoppable
5	**A** involve	**B** pay	**C** interact	**D** have
6	**A** locates	**B** builds	**C** houses	**D** provides
7	**A** grounds	**B** location	**C** area	**D** landscape
8	**A** ride	**B** drive	**C** mount	**D** trek
9	**A** Crafts	**B** Refreshments	**C** Wildlife	**D** Sights
10	**A** entry	**B** enter	**C** entrance	**D** exit
11	**A** open	**B** subject	**C** according	**D** able
12	**A** venue	**B** thrill	**C** settlement	**D** leisure

2 Read the text below. Use the words given in capitals at the end of each line to form a word that fits in the same line. There is an example at the beginning **(0)**.

Sussex in Miniature is a spectacular **(0)** .collection. of handcrafted Sussex	COLLECT
landmarks which are beautifully recreated in two acres of **(1)**	DELIGHT
walled gardens with fountains and waterfalls. **(2)**	ENTERTAIN
for all the family, where visitors can **(3)** .... the history	JOY
of Sussex with its **(4)** .... castles and railways of the	SPECTACLE
past. At Paradise Park, the exhibits are **(5)** .... changing	CONTINUE
through the seasons with new displays being added each year. The gardens	
were created to provide awareness of the need for **(6)**	CONSERVE
of the world's **(7)** .... The Secrets of Planet Earth is one of	ATTRACT
the finest **(8)** .... of its type in the country and is home to	EXHIBIT
a collection of fascinating fossils. An **(9)** .... show involving	ACT
the audience brings the feature to life. This is a truly **(10)**	PLEASURE
day out for all the family.	

1a Complete the table with the correct words from the box. Some words can fit in more than one category.

> account   afford   bargain   borrow   display   earn   entertainment   facilities
> goods   interest   lend   owe   picnic   play area   refreshments   refund
> safari park   sale   shop around   try on   window-shopping

Money	Shopping	Leisure

b Complete the following short texts with the words from **a**. Make any necessary changes.

1 I go to the shops in town with my best friend every weekend. If we're short of money, we just spend our time (1) ...., or we look for (2) .... like CDs or clothes at reduced prices. It's quite amazing how much money you can save if you're prepared to (3) .... I once went into a shop with a friend who (4) .... a really nice summer jacket. It was lucky she didn't buy it, because we walked into another shop and saw exactly the same jacket reduced by 20 per cent. Of course, there can be a problem with buying (5) .... at reduced prices – some shops don't offer a (6) .... to customers who want to return something they bought in a (7) ....

2 I really wanted to buy a new car and I had my eye on one which cost £15,000. I had just over £7,000 in my bank (1) ...., so I needed (2) .... £8,000, which was quite a large amount for me because I don't (3) .... a lot of money in my job. The bank manager worked out that the loan would cost me nearly £400 a month, including the (4) .... I would have to pay. She asked me if I could really (5) .... such a big loan, but, in the end, she did agree to (6) .... me the money. I am now the proud owner of a new car. I still (7) .... the bank quite a lot of money, but I think it's worth it to have such a great car.

3 For a successful day out, it is important that you choose somewhere that provides (1) .... for everyone on the trip. Last year, we went to a (2) .... where we enjoyed seeing the animals running free right next to our car. There was also an excellent (3) .... there for younger children where our four-year-old son had a great time. Our older children enjoyed looking at a wonderful (4) .... that gave all kinds of information about the animals and their natural environments. After all that, we were all ready for some (5) .... We sat and had a (6) .... in the beautiful gardens and then looked at the rest of the grounds. Everything was very clean and all the staff were very helpful; all in all, we were really impressed by the (7) .... on offer to the public.

c Choose the best heading from the list (A–F) for each of the texts (1–3) in **b**.

A Fun for the whole family **D** Keeping children entertained

B Shopping without cash **E** Sensible shopping

C A car I shouldn't have bought **F** Getting what you want sooner

2 Read the text below. Use the word given in capitals at the end of each line to form a word that fits in the space in the same line. There is an example at the beginning **(0)**.

Most people probably think that being a **(0)** ......*manager*...... of a leisure centre is a   MANAGE

(1) .... job and an easy way of making a living. In reality, it is one of the   WONDER

most **(2)** .... jobs imaginable. Having done this job myself, I can say from   DEMAND

experience that there are two **(3)** .... qualities which you must have to   PERSON

make a success of the job. The first is **(4)** .... You are in charge of a large   EFFICIENT

organisation and anyone who was **(5)** .... would soon find themselves in   ORGANISE

a dreadful mess. The next is **(6)** .... You have a lot of staff under you   CHEERFUL

who often need your **(7)** .... and help, particularly when dealing with   ENCOURAGE

the public. Some clients can be difficult or even **(8)** .... to a centre's   ABUSE

(9) .... if they are upset about something. A manager who is able to step   EMPLOY

in and sort the problem out with a smile is far more **(10)** .... than one   EFFECT

who shows the staff or the public that he or she is under stress.

3 Read the text below and decide which answer **A**, **B**, **C** or **D** best fits each space.

I find that working in the clothing department of a good quality store is a **(1)** .... and interesting job. I started in the department where I work as a sales assistant, but last year I was **(2)** .... and put **(3)** .... charge of the department. Since I have been running the department, I have tried to strike a balance between the quite **(4)** .... clothes we carry and the very up-to-date, 'trendier' styles. We have customers with a range of tastes and I **(5)** .... pleasure in knowing that we manage to satisfy the needs of all of them. It is of course essential to display the clothes **(6)** ...., so that the customers will find them appealing. I also have to make sure that my **(7)** .... are professional in their approach to their work. On the one hand, good salespeople have to be **(8)** .... but, at the same time, they have to have plenty of patience. It can be very frustrating when customers change their **(9)** .... several times before they finally buy something. There are times when every salesperson just has to hold their **(10)** .... because some customers can be irritating. Having said that, I must admit that the majority of our customers are polite and very **(11)** .... of the quality of service we offer. **(12)** .... far the most difficult time for us is the sales period, when the department is full of shoppers who are determined to take **(13)** .... of the special prices. We just don't stop all day long and at times we all wonder how we are going to **(14)** .... through the day. When the sales are over, though, the department quietens down and we can take a **(15)** ....

1	A various	B varied	C mixed	D different
2	A promoted	B advanced	C raised	D upgraded
3	A on	B with	C at	D in
4	A original	B traditional	C typical	D old
5	A have	B feel	C take	D hold
6	A attractively	B beautifully	C efficiently	D successfully
7	A workers	B employers	C staff	D people
8	A persuasive	B persuading	C pushing	D decisive
9	A views	B minds	C decisions	D opinions
10	A breathe	B mouth	C tongue	D words
11	A grateful	B appreciative	C admiring	D pleased
12	A So	B At	C By	D In
13	A opportunity	B chance	C advantage	D benefit
14	A go	B get	C survive	D manage
15	A break	B rest	C relaxation	D vacations

Developing reading skills

Lead-in

1a Match the names of the animals (1–10) with the pictures (A–J).

1 hamster
2 husky
3 parrot
4 kitten
5 pony
6 python
7 lizard
8 tropical fish
9 tortoise
10 terrapin

b Which of the animals in **a** would make good pets for you in the place where you live? Why?
Which ones would you not like to keep as pets? Why?

2 Make statements about the advantages and disadvantages of the following animals as pets,
choosing suitable information from the table.

e.g. *Hamsters are easy to look after and they don't take up much space.*

Hamsters are cheap to keep but you can't do much with them.

animals	advantages	disadvantages
horses	are cheap to keep	can disturb neighbours
large dogs	don't take up much space	are expensive to keep
snakes	require little equipment	require a lot of space
hamsters	are clean to have in the home	can make a mess in the home
cats	aren't destructive	require a lot of equipment
fish	make good companions	need a lot of exercise
parrots	are easy to look after	can do serious damage
small dogs	are beautiful and fascinating	you can't do much with them

3 Match the beginnings of the advertisements (1–4) with the correct endings (a–d).

1 Let us take good care of your dog

2 Bring your children to us

3 Choose your tropical fish

4 Switch to our range of specially-balanced foods

a from more than fifty species we have on display

b to ensure your pets stay fit and healthy

c while you're away on holiday

d when they ask for horse-riding lessons

Reading task: Multiple matching (headings)

Strategy: Understanding the gist (the main idea) of a paragraph

1a Skim through the first paragraph of the following text on looking after horses. You will see that the heading is missing.

1

Think carefully before you rush out and buy that appealing little pony or that wonderful-looking horse. As anyone who has ever owned one of these animals will tell you, they are affectionate creatures that you become very attached to, but their upkeep is considerable. It's not just a question of paying for their stabling and feed. If you are unlucky enough to have an animal that is prone to injuries, vets' bills can become a major headache. Bear in mind that an operation on a horse can cost more than a similar operation on a human being. Bear in mind also that children can be enthusiastic in the beginning and quickly tire of the constant effort it takes to look after a horse.

b Look back at the above paragraph and at the headings **A–E** below. Decide which of the headings best describes the gist (the main idea) of the paragraph.

A They are not worth the expense

B Choose your horse carefully

C Don't buy a horse

D A serious commitment

E Medical bills can be high

c Underline the phrases in the paragraph in **a** that helped you choose the correct heading. Underline any headings you rejected because they focused on details and not on the gist of the paragraph.

tip

Be careful not to choose headings just because they repeat words you find in the text. Just because they use the same word does not mean that they describe the gist of the paragraph.

2a Skim through the next two paragraphs from the same text. Choose the most suitable heading from the list **A–D** each time.

2

Horses and ponies are large animals that require regular exercise. If they don't get the exercise they need, they become stressed and difficult to handle. This means that you need plenty of space to exercise them in. If you are lucky enough to own land that is large enough to keep an animal on, you should take expert advice before you set about building the stable where it will live. Even if you have the space, you might still be better advised to keep your horse in a professionally-run stable. Your children can learn to ride there and, later, to jump. You should also be aware that if you want your children to take part in competitions, you will need a horsebox to transport the animal in.

A Having the right facilities

B Exercising the horse

C Avoiding stressing the animal

D Getting professional help with your horse

3

A horse or a pony should be kept in warm and clean conditions. It should also be examined regularly by a vet and vaccinated against a number of diseases that horses are prone to. Small injuries should be treated immediately before they develop into major problems. And don't forget that a horse needs a carefully-balanced diet, if you want to have a healthy animal. It also requires regular grooming to keep its coat looking shiny and healthy.

A The right equipment

B The right care

C The right conditions

D The right medical care

b Which heading(s) repeated a word in the text but did not describe the gist of paragraph 2 and 3?

Exam practice: Part 1

You are going to read a text about a breed of dog which is becoming popular as a pet. Choose the most suitable heading from the list **A–I** for each part **(1–7)** of the text. There is one extra heading which you do not need to use. There is an example at the beginning **(0)**.

Remember!

Remember to focus on the gist of each paragraph when matching the headings. You will also need to use other strategies.

A The difficulties of the breed

B Care of the dog

C Great dogs to own

D The origins of the breed

E The appeal of huskies

F The character of huskies

G Training huskies

H Competition dogs

I The right owners

exam tip

You may find unfamiliar words in the reading text in the exam. Ignore these words if they do not prevent you understanding the gist of each paragraph.

Owning a husky

0   **D**

Just a few years ago, Siberian huskies were virtually unknown outside North America, but their popularity is rapidly growing elsewhere, particularly in some European countries. Originally bred by a Siberian people called the Chukchi to pull their sledges, huskies are thought to be descended from dogs that were crossed with wolves. This would explain an unusual characteristic of the breed which is that huskies do not bark like other dogs but howl, especially when they are left on their own.

1

Siberian huskies are among the most beautiful of dogs. They are a compact but strong-looking dog with a neat coat and a large bushy tail that is usually held erect. The most striking aspect of many huskies is their vivid blue eyes, although many have dark brown eyes; some even have one blue and one brown eye. They are also noted for the elegant way they move, with their heads held high, always curious about what is going on around them. Husky puppies look just like soft toys.

2

They are one of the friendliest breeds of dogs and one reason for their increasing popularity is their reputation as dogs that can be trusted with small children. Indeed, many owners report that their dogs insist on joining in their children's games. They cannot stand being ignored, something that can be a problem when guests arrive and a husky is unable to understand that the guests have really come to chat with its owner, not to spend the whole evening playing with a dog. This friendliness does not extend to other dogs, however. Males can be aggressive when they encounter other dogs, especially males of the same breed.

3

Huskies were bred to run over great distances without tiring and they can pull three times their own weight. As anyone who has ever taken one of these dogs for a walk will tell you, the instinct to pull is very strong in them. Getting them to stop pulling on the lead is very difficult, if not impossible. If they don't get sufficient exercise, they can become destructive in the house. They have remarkably strong teeth and can chew through almost anything, including expensive furniture. Anyone thinking of buying one of these dogs should also realise that twice a year they shed a huge amount of hair that gets everywhere in the house.

4

Huskies are dogs for fit and active people who are prepared to put a lot of time in exercising their animal. Anyone whose idea of walking a dog is a gentle stroll around the block a couple of times a day should get a different breed. Ideally, huskies should be let off the lead for an hour or more several times a week so that they can run off their energy. People who have access to open spaces where the dog is not likely to run across a road and get killed will, therefore, find these dogs easier to deal with than people who live in crowded city areas.

5

Despite the difficulties involved in owning one of these dogs, huskies are in some ways easy to look after. For one thing, they are particularly clean dogs. For another, their thick coat requires little attention. A twice-weekly brushing is all that is needed to keep them looking neat. Their coat does seem to benefit if an oil supplement is added to their diet, possibly because in their native Siberia they would have been fed on seal meat and fish; in other words, on a diet rich in animal oil.

6

Huskies have long been used in Alaska in sledge-pulling races. In parts of Europe that lack snow for all or part of the year, enthusiastic owners have come up with an ingenious way of racing huskies in snowless conditions. Instead of sledges, teams of huskies pull wheeled vehicles in races. This is a great activity for parents and children to take part in together. The dogs themselves enjoy every minute of it.

7

As anyone who has had a husky from a puppy knows, these dogs are extremely loyal to their owners. The affection with which a husky greets its owner when he or she has been out of the house for just an hour or so is remarkable. They may not be the easiest dogs in the world to walk, but just take one into a park or along the road and you can be sure that several people will stop you to ask about the dog and ask if they can stroke it. They are dogs that people seem to be irresistibly attracted to.

Language development

Word attack

1 Look back at the text on p.59. Find the words that mean the same as the following definitions.

 1 to make the short, loud sound that dogs make ....

 2 eager to know something or learn about something ....

 3 young dogs ....

 4 always ready to argue or attack ....

 5 a type of animal, dog, etc. ....

 6 a natural tendency or ability to behave or react in a certain way ....

 7 a piece of leather, rope, etc. fastened to a dog's collar in order to control it

 ....

 8 to bite something repeatedly ....

 9 a feeling of love or caring ....

 10 to move your hand gently over something ....

2 Complete the following text, using the words from **Exercise 1**. Make any necessary changes.

Last year, my dog gave birth to four beautiful little (1) .... Because the father was a different (2) .... from her, two of them looked like her and the other two were completely different. We were (3) .... to see whether she would treat all four in the same way. In fact, she treated them all with great (4) .... and she was a very good mother. The only problem was that because of her (5) .... to protect them she started to become quite (6) .... with us. Whenever we went near any of them, she would start (7) .... at us. We found the best thing to do was to give her a bone to (8) .... on to relax her, then she would let us pick up all four of her young and (9) .... them.

Phrasal verbs

Complete the following short texts, using the correct form of the phrasal verbs in the box. Make any necessary changes. Use each phrasal verb once only.

> **bring back   bring into   clean out   find out   get on   go without   grow up**
> **look after   put up with   run after   set up   settle down   take out   take up   tie up**

1 Giving children small animals like hamsters and rabbits (1) .... is a good way for them to learn responsibility. They have to understand that the animals' cages need (2) .... regularly and that their pets cannot (3) .... fresh water and food for long or they will die.

2 People who are thinking of (1) .... tropical fish breeding should (2) .... as much about the subject as they can before they start. It is essential that an aquarium (3) .... properly so that the fish have the right conditions to breed in.

3 A dog that (1) .... on the end of a chain or a rope all day becomes unhappy and aggressive. It should (2) .... at least once a day. Owners should regard this as a chance to have fun with the dog. The dog can be encouraged (3) .... a ball and then rewarded when the ball (4) ....

4 Cats and dogs can (1) .... well with each other if they (2) .... together. However, a cat that is (3) .... a house where there already is a dog will never be able to (4) .... and the dog will never learn to (5) .... the cat.

Word-building: adjectives

1 Complete the table with adjectives formed from the words in the box.

> adventure courage curl dirt drink filth fun help manage meaning
> monotony nerve pain replace rest ridicule risk tire wash

care**less**	break**able**	bush**y**	danger**ous**

2 Complete the following sentences with adjectives ending in *-ful* or *-less* formed from the words in the box.

> care help pain rest use

1a The people in that pet shop are very .... They're always willing to give advice.

b There is no worse sight than a .... animal which is in pain.

2a You have to be very .... when handling some tropical fish because they are poisonous.

b .... people who leave broken glass in the streets cause a lot of injuries to dogs and cats.

3a I find looking at fish swimming silently in an aquarium very ....

b Animals like lions and tigers become very .... if they are kept in small cages.

4a Our dog had a very .... injury when it was hit by a car.

b The vet assured us that the injection she was giving our cat would be completely .... and the cat wouldn't feel a thing.

5a He's kept fish for years and he can give you some very .... tips about how to look after them.

b There are a lot of good pet accessories on the market but there are also some which are utterly .... and a complete waste of money.

Use of English

Read the text below. Use the words given in capitals at the end of each line to form a word that fits in the same line. There is an example at the beginning **(0)**.

In the holidays, my family visited a **(0)** ...*famous*.... zoo. I enjoyed seeing the elephants the FAME
most, although the place where they were kept was quite **(1)** .... All of us SMELL
agreed that the pandas were the most **(2)** .... animals in the zoo. By far ADORE
the **(3)** .... part of the zoo was the aviary where there were many different NOISE
species of birds. It was a **(4)** .... building, large enough to allow the birds MARVEL
to fly freely around it. The zoo had many insect and arachnid species, including large
(5) .... spiders which fascinated my brother. Their keeper said that they HAIR
were so **(6)** .... that one bite from them could kill a person. However, he POISON
seemed quite **(7)** .... when he handled them. All the keepers at the zoo FEAR
were very **(8)** .... about the animals they looked after. Of course, visitors KNOWLEDGE
to any zoo should behave in a **(9)** .... way. One of the keepers told us that REASON
recently some **(10)** .... person nearly killed an animal by giving it THOUGHT
unsuitable food.

Developing reading skills

Lead-in

1 Talk about how the people in the family tree are related to each other, using the words in the box.

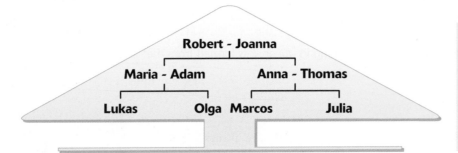

husband   wife
son   daughter
grandson   granddaughter
cousin   uncle   aunt
niece   nephew
brother-in-law   sister-in-law

2 Work with a partner and answer the following questions.

- Do you get on well with everyone in your family? Which members of your family do you have a particularly close relationship with?

- Which of your relations do you often see? Which do you rarely see? Are there any you have never seen?

- Did you grow up in a large or small family? Is the size of the average family in your country growing or getting smaller? Do you know why?

Reading task: Multiple choice

Strategy: Looking for reference sentences

> **tip**
>
> You will often meet sentences that refer back to important information contained earlier in the text. These reference sentences can help you work out the answers to some of the multiple-choice questions. Reference sentences usually – but not always – contain words like *this, that, these, those,* etc.

1 Match the sentences (a–d) with the statements they refer back to (1–4).

1 I grew up in a huge family and I helped my mother look after the younger children. It never crossed my mind to complain about having to do this. As kids, we all knew we had to help out.

2 I was an only child and my parents gave me everything. They worried about me all the time and they were very selective about the children they would allow me to play with.

3 When I was a child we lived really well. We had a beautiful house, a maid and expensive foreign holidays. My parents never saved a penny. Then my father lost his job. After that, we were always terribly short of money and I couldn't go to college because I had to go out and get a job.

4 I was very close to my grandparents when I was growing up. They used to take me out and buy me things and tell me all kinds of stories which I loved listening to.

a All that made me a rather nervous and selfish person, if I'm honest.

b This is why I feel it is very important that my children should spend time with my own parents.

c That's the kind of upbringing which teaches you to get on well with other people and to be unselfish.

d That experience showed me how important it is to look after your money.

2 Read the following paragraphs of a text about a person's upbringing and answer the multiple-choice questions.

I grew up in a small industrial town. My parents both worked in a nearby factory. Few families in the town were well-off but most of us were content with our lives. More than anything, it was the closeness of our families that kept us happy. On Sundays, everyone would put on their best clothes and go out to visit relatives and friends. All of us were brought up to understand the importance of our families to us and we developed a strong sense of belonging to the community we grew up in. *Those values have stayed with me throughout my life.*

1 What do the words *those values* in the above sentence in *italics* refer to?

A respecting your family and the people around you

B being happy to work in a factory all your life

C keeping in touch with relatives as well as with friends

D wearing respectable clothes when you go out on Sundays

Although our town was industrial, it was surrounded by beautiful unspoilt country. As a child, I spent hours on end playing with my brothers and sisters, cousins and friends in the woods around the town, catching fish in a nearby river and, in the summer, swimming in the freezing water. We would all rush out of the house after breakfast, appear briefly for our lunch, which we ate as fast as we possibly could, and then we would be off again out of the house to meet our friends. By the evening, we were so tired that we couldn't stay awake and had to be carried to bed by our parents. *I often wish my own children could have grown up like that.*

2 What do the words *like that* in the above sentence in *italics* refer to?

A living in an industrial area

B being free to go out and play all day

C having a river nearby

D being tired and ready to go to bed early

My parents couldn't afford to send me to college so I had to get a job. Like most of my relatives, I went to work in a local factory. I was assigned to the accounts office where one of my uncles worked. I knew I would have to wait years to get a good position there. Many people, including my parents, told me I was lucky to have got a job in that department because there were a lot of people unemployed. *I knew I could never look at life in this way.* After just six months in the job, I walked out.

3 What does the phrase *look at life in this way* in the above sentence in *italics* refer to?

A wanting to work with your relatives

B accepting that you cannot go to college

C wanting to have a high position

D being satisfied with whatever you have got

I moved to a city in the south of the country where, after a lot of hard work, I built up a whole business empire. Today, I am one of the richest people in the country. I have children of my own now, who I send to an expensive private school. I have seen most parts of the world and I own several houses, racehorses and a private collection of classic cars. On the other hand, I often remember how happy I was while I was growing up. *Then I wonder if such things are, in the end, all that important.*

4 What do the words *such things* in the above sentence in *italics* refer to?

A moving to another part of the country

B the experiences of your childhood

C living the typical lifestyle of a wealthy person

D being able to give children a private education

Exam practice: Part 2

You are going to read an extract from a book in which a famous writer recalls the time he left home.
For Questions **1–8**, choose the answer (**A**, **B**, **C** or **D**) which you think fits best according to the text.

Remember!

Remember to look for reference sentences and the information in the text that they refer back to. You will also need to use other strategies.

The stooping figure of my mother, waist-deep in the grass and caught there like a piece of sheep's wool, was the last I saw of my country home as I left it to discover the world. She stood old and bent at the top of the bank, silently watching me go, one hand raised in farewell and blessing, not questioning why I went. At the bend of the road I looked back again and saw her; then I turned the corner and walked out of the village. I had closed that part of my life for ever.

It was a bright Sunday morning in early June, the right time to be leaving home. We had been a close family who always got on well together but my three sisters and a brother had already gone. There were two other brothers who had not yet got around to making a decision. They were still sleeping that morning, but my mother had got up early and cooked me a heavy breakfast, had stood wordlessly while I ate it, her hand on my chair, and had then helped me pack up my few belongings. There had been no fuss; there had been no attempt to persuade me to stay; she just gave me a long and searching look. Then, with my bags on my back, I'd gone out into the early sunshine and climbed through the long wet grass to the road.

It was 1934. I was nineteen years old, still soft at the edges, but with a confident belief in good fortune. I carried a small rolled-up tent, a violin in a blanket, a change of clothes, a tin of biscuits, and some cheese. I was excited, full of self-confidence, knowing I had far to go; but not, as yet, how far. I left home that morning and walked away from the sleeping village. It never crossed my mind that others had done this before me.

And now I was on my journey at last, in a thick pair of boots and a stick in my hand. Naturally, I was going to London, which lay a hundred miles to the east; and it seemed equally obvious that I should go on foot. But first, as I'd never seen the sea, I thought I'd try to walk to the coast and find it. This would add another hundred miles to my journey. It would also cost me several extra days of walking. Such considerations didn't trouble me, however. I felt that I'd get by, whatever happened.

That first day alone – and now I was really on my own at last – steadily declined in excitement. Through the solitary morning and afternoon I found myself longing for hurrying footsteps coming after me and family voices calling me back.

None came. I was free. The day's silence said, 'Go where you will. It's all yours. You asked for it. It's up to you now.' As I walked I was followed by thoughts of home, by the tinkling sounds of the kitchen, shafts of sun from the windows falling across familiar furniture, across the bedroom and the bed I had left.

When I judged it to be tea-time I sat on an old stone wall and opened my tin of biscuits. As I ate them, I could almost hear mother making tea and my brothers rattling their tea-cups. The biscuits tasted sweetly of home – still only a dozen miles away.

I might have turned back then if it hadn't been for my brothers, but I knew I could never have put up with the teasing I would have got from them. So I went on my way.

When darkness came, I was too weary to put up the tent. So I lay down in the middle of a field and stared up at the brilliant stars. Finally, the smells of the night put me to sleep – my first night without a roof or bed.

I was awoken soon after midnight by drizzling rain on my face. I was cold and the sky was black and the stars had all gone. Two cows stood over me, moaning in the darkness. Those memories have stayed with me ever since. But when the sun rose in the morning, the birds were singing. I got up, shook myself, ate a piece of pie, and turned again to the south.

1 The writer left his home feeling that
   A he would soon be back to continue his life in the village.
   B life outside the village would be difficult.
   C he could not stand the smallness of the village any longer.
   D this was the end of an important part of his life.

2 In the writer's family
   A the rest of the children were still living at home.
   B all the other children had left home.
   C the boys had left but the girls had stayed.
   D some of the boys had stayed but the rest of the children had left.

3 Before the writer left the house, his mother
   A had looked at him to be sure that he really wanted to go.
   B had let him make his own preparations to leave.
   C had helped him to prepare for the journey but asked him not to go.
   D had tried to persuade him to take his brothers with him.

4 As he walked out of the village, the writer felt
   A sadness about leaving his mother.
   B excitement about all the opportunities ahead of him.
   C that many generations of young men had done the same thing before.
   D that he should hurry because of the long journey in front of him.

5 The writer
   A was worried that he might not find his way to the sea.
   B did not care if he used time and energy to go to the sea.
   C did not care if he did not get to London after all.
   D wondered if he could walk all the way to London.

6 On the first day of his journey, the writer
   A was followed by his brothers who asked him to come back.
   B stopped for a meal only when he was a long way from home.
   C did not turn back because his brothers would think he had failed.
   D was thoroughly happy that he was finally free.

7 What the writer most clearly remembers about his first night alone is
   A seeing two cows in a field.
   B lying in bed and looking at the stars.
   C having difficulty putting up his tent.
   D waking up feeling wet and miserable.

8 The extract shows the writer looks back on his experience and
   A regrets wasting so much time as a young man.
   B feels a strong sense of love for his mother.
   C feels he should go back and live in the village.
   D is glad he does not live in the village any more.

Language development

Word attack

1 Look back at the text on p.64. Find the words and expressions that mean the same as the following definitions.

1 had a friendly relationship ....

2 found the time ....

3 the thought occurred to me ....

4 walk ....

5 manage, whatever the difficulties ....

6 alone, with no one to turn to for help ....

7 returned in the same direction ....

8 accept something unpleasant without complaining ....

2 Complete the following text using the words and expressions from **Exercise 1**. Make any necessary changes.

Even in families where parents and children (1) .... with each other, there can be some arguments when the children become teenagers. Parents find it difficult to (2) .... the bad moods some teenagers have.

On the other hand, many parents seldom (3) .... sitting with their teenage children to talk to them about their problems. It never (4) .... of many teenagers that their parents were once teenagers themselves and they might be able to give them some helpful advice. Some parents, of course, worry a lot about their children's future, while the children just assume they will (5) .... in whatever they decide to do. Parents look at their teenage children's relaxed attitude to life and wonder if they will be able to survive (6) .... after they have left home.

Compounds beginning with *self-*

1 Look at the example from the text on p.64.

*I was excited, full of **self-confidence** …*

2 Complete the following sentences, using the compounds with *self-* in the box.

self-catering	self-centred	self-confidence	self-defence	self-discipline
	self-employed	self-reliant	self-service	

1 My family like eating in .... restaurants because they are cheap and informal.

2 I want my children to learn some .... techniques, just in case they are ever in danger.

3 Children without brothers and sisters can become .... if their parents give them everything they want.

4 We like staying in .... holiday flats because we like to eat whenever we want to.

5 My father is .... He works for himself, not for a company.

6 Parents should help their children to gain .... by praising them when they do well.

7 Children have to develop .... so that they can study efficiently.

8 They wanted their children to grow up to become .... rather than being dependent on them.

Compound nouns: family relationships

1 Give one word to describe each of the following family relationships (1–5). Use the prefixes and suffix *half-, great-, step-, ex-* and *-in-law*.

  1 the father of the man a woman has married

  2 a man who is not a child's natural father but who their mother has married

  3 a sister related to another child through only one of their parents

  4 the woman who a man used to be married to but isn't married to any more

  5 the grandfather of someone's father or mother

2 Complete the following interview with a woman called Susan, using the compound nouns from **Exercise 1** and the phrasal verbs in the box. Use each compound noun and phrasal verb once only.

> **bring up   grow up   look down on**
> **take after   take care of   take to**

Interviewer: Susan, you (1) .... in a huge old castle in Scotland. I imagine you were quite a well-off family

Susan: Oh, yes. My (2) .... on my father's side of the family had made a fortune, back in the nineteenth century. Then my mother's father had done well in business, too.

Interviewer: So your father was already wealthy when he married, and then he also had a (3) .... who had made a lot of money.

Susan: Yes, that's right. We were lucky, really.

Interviewer: I suppose you must (4) .... in a pretty traditional, conservative way?

Susan: Not really. My mother taught my brother and me that we should never (5) .... people who were less fortunate than ourselves.

Interviewer: Do you think you (6) .... your mother or your father?

Susan: My mother. Her respect for people has stayed with me all my life and I know I think like her. Unfortunately my father was killed in the war when I was was quite young.

Interviewer: Did your mother remarry?

Susan: Yes, she did, so my brother and I had to get used to having a (7) ....

Interviewer: Was that difficult?

Susan: Not really, because we (8) .... him straightaway. He was a kind man who showed us a lot of love and (9) .... us as if we had been his own children. When he married my mother, he already had a daughter but she was often away, staying down in London with his (10) ....

Interviewer: So, he had already been married once before when he married your mother?

Susan: Yes, that's right. So, he sort of inherited us, then he and my mother had a child together, a girl, so I have a brother and a (11) ....

Some uses of *leave*

1 Look at the example from the text on p.64.

  … the right time to be
  leaving home*.*

| home |
| school |
| a job, a company, etc. |
| a country, a village, etc. |

leave

| a decision to someone |
| a message |

| money/property to somebody |

| somebody/something behind |
| somebody/something alone |

2 Complete the following text, using the correct form of *leave* and appropriate words or expressions from the boxes.

I met my best friend and some other friends in a pub a few evenings ago. We were going on to a club but my best friend didn't want to come so, in the end, we (1) .... her .... in the pub. The next day, I phoned her house and (2) .... with her brother for her to call me back. She didn't, and when I finally got through to her, she just told me (3) .... her .... and put the phone down. I went round to her house to find out what was the matter with her.

She told me that she (4) .... her .... just a few days before, after working there for just over a month. She was starting to regret (5) .... the year before, because she had no qualifications to help her to get a decent job. She even criticised her parents for (6) .... the .... to her about whether she should stay on at school or not. Some people are never satisfied!

Developing reading skills

Lead-in

1 Look at the picture below and answer the questions.

BACK IN 2 HOURS

1 Why might this house be an invitation to a burglar or thief?

2 What kind of things might be stolen?

3 What do you think the saying 'Opportunity makes the thief' means?

2 Match the crimes in the box below to the descriptions (1–10).

arson   burglary   forgery   hijacking   mugging   pickpocketing   robbery
shoplifting   smuggling   vandalism

1 I caught him just as he was taking my wallet from my back pocket.

....

2 The gang was arrested while trying to get diamonds and drugs into the country illegally. ....

3 Terrorists ordered the pilot to fly the plane to another country. ....

4 The teenagers smashed windows and sprayed graffiti on the walls of the youth centre. ....

5 The thieves held the bank manager at gun-point while they took the cash.

....

6 When he broke the back window to get in, our alarm went off. ....

7 He was found guilty of copying classic paintings and trying to sell them as originals. ....

8 The gang of youths was arrested for attacking the woman and taking her handbag.

....

9 Two young girls were found guilty of taking the item from the supermarket without paying for it. ....

10 He had set fire to the forest just for fun. ....

Reading task: Gapped text

Strategy: Understanding the connection between two ideas – cause and effect

> **tip**
>
> Look for words and phrases which connect two ideas in a sentence or paragraph, e.g. *She was driving fast **because** she was late for an appointment.*

1a Read the following text on crime, focusing on how the words in *italics* link the text.

The British public is getting worried, *because* crimes like theft and burglary and violent crimes are on the increase. *As a result*, the government has decided to take tough measures on all types of crime, including relatively petty offences, and has created legislation which gives more power to the courts.

The effect of the new law was seen recently when a young man gave his girlfriend a pair of earrings for her birthday. He had bought the items from a street trader without knowing where they had come from. They had been stolen. Due to his ignorance, he was arrested for handling stolen goods and was put in a police cell.

In the eyes of the law in Britain, there's no difference between what the young man did and what the average thief or burglar does with their loot. The young man was guilty of handling goods which had been stolen and *so* he was breaking the law.

In court, the judge said he would use the case to deter others and consequently, the youth is now serving a nine-month prison sentence. 'Anybody who deals in anything that has been stolen is committing an offence,' said the judge. 'Legally, there is no difference between stealing something yourself or having it in your possession. Possession of stolen goods can result in the individual being charged and convicted.'

From the above case, it is clear that the government has decided to crack down on all forms of crime and has instructed judges not to show leniency to those breaking the law. 'Criminals must know that if they get caught, juries are likely to be harsh and *therefore* jail terms will be long,' said a government spokesperson.

b Read the text again and answer the following questions.

1 What is the effect of the increase in crime in Britain?

2 The government has decided to create legislation as a result of what?

3 Why was the young man arrested?

4 What other words or expressions are used in the text to express cause and effect? Find two examples.

2 Complete the following sentences with words or expressions which link the effect of something to its cause. Sometimes more than one answer is possible.

1 The gangster was found guilty of murder and as .... he was sent to prison for 25 years.

2 We didn't have any locks on the windows and .... it was easy for the burglar to break in.

3 .... his previous record, the vandal was sent to a young offender's institute for six months.

4 There weren't any witnesses to the robbery. ...., the police are making slow progress with the case.

Exam practice: Part 3

You are going to read an article about crimes against property. Eight sentences have been removed from the article. Choose from the sentences **A–I** the one which fits each gap **(1–7)**. There is one extra sentence which you do not need to use. There is an example at the beginning **(0)**.

> **Remember!**
>
> Remember to look for words and expressions that show cause and effect when choosing the correct sentence. You will also need to use other strategies.

Crimes against property

In recent years, there has been an explosion of property-related crimes in almost every country. Despite what the majority of people think, such crime is not committed by professional criminals, nor is it carefully planned. **0** **E** However, it is surprising how many people still fail to take sensible steps to protect their property and belongings.

In the case of preventing theft from the home, this can be easily done by installing alarms or fitting strong locks on all points of access to the house. **1** Additionally, intruders are seldom keen to try their luck on buildings where there are signs of life. **2** This may be as simple as leaving a light or television on while you are out.

As most burglaries are committed by adolescents and young men living within two or three kilometres of the victim, they tend to have a good knowledge of the area and are constantly on the lookout for the telltale signs of empty premises. Amazingly, in three out of ten break-ins, the thief does not even have to use force to get in because the householder has left a door unlocked or a window open. **3**

While not quite in the same league as theft and burglary, there has also been a huge increase in vandalism and the destruction of property. One area of the community badly affected by vandalism is schools – for example, between five and ten per cent of some education authorities' maintenance budgets is spent repairing deliberate damage. **4**

Another very visible form of property crime is the writing and spray-painting which plagues many city walls. Graffiti has long been identified as one of the major causes of the fear of crime among many city residents. **5** If it is widespread, it may even reduce tourism for similar reasons.

The vandals themselves, on the other hand, take great pleasure in graffiti because of the notoriety and kudos it may generate for them, and although some murals display a great amount of talent on the part of the artist, more common are the unattractive tags, or 'signatures'. **6** The offenders normally plan their strikes carefully and because it doesn't take them long to spray their messages, they are rarely apprehended by the police. **7**

Despite the depressing statistics associated with property crime, greater cooperation between police, schools, businesses and the local community as a whole will help in the fight to reduce it.

A If opportunities like these did not exist, criminals would have a much harder time and many crimes would not be committed at all.

B Their acts resulted in the arrests of several burglars and vandals.

C This is because people often associate it with the presence of street gangs and consequently may become afraid to frequent or use those public spaces where it is prevalent.

D As a result, they seldom have convictions or a police record.

E In fact, it is the work of opportunists and theoretically, therefore, should be easy to prevent.

F These are sprayed on as many places as possible and often refer to the gang or 'crew' to which the culprit belongs.

G So the police often advise to try to give the impression that someone is at home.

H The money could be used elsewhere by reducing vandalism through good design, sensible security measures and better management.

I Burglars shy away from doors and windows which are properly secured as these can be difficult to open.

tip

Understanding linking words can help you to deal with unknown vocabulary in a specific sentence or paragraph.

Language development

Word attack

1 Phrasal verbs can sometimes be used as nouns. Look at the example from the text on p.70.

*Amazingly, in three out of ten **break-ins**, ...*

2 Complete the following sentences, using the words in the box.

> **breakout   crackdown   drawback   getaway   giveaway
> hold-up   set-up   setback   telling-off**

1 The main .... of city life is the high risk of being a victim
of a crime.

2 The bank robbers made their .... in a stolen car.

3 Undercover police had set a trap for a local gangster, but he realised it was
a .... and drove off before he made contact.

4 The teacher gave the boy a .... for defacing the school walls.

5 There was a .... at the bank yesterday afternoon and the
robbers got away with a huge amount of money.

6 Three prisoners went on the run after a .... but were
recaptured after being spotted by members of the public.

7 There has been a .... by the police on drug trafficking.

8 Being arrested for drunken driving was a .... to his career as
a judge.

9 He had been drinking whisky and his glazed eyes were a dead
....

Connectors: cause and effect

Complete the following text, using the words and expressions in the box.
Sometimes more than one answer is possible.

> **as a result   because of   consequently
> due to   so   so that   therefore**

There are many reasons for crime. Social scientists suggest that criminal behaviour is
(1) .... social issues like unemployment, poor housing and lack of
education. (2) ...., they suggest that we can only fight crime by turning
our attention to such issues and (3) .... help to improve society in general.

Others believe that people should take responsibility for their actions and that crime
cannot be excused (4) .... poverty or lack of education. Such people argue
that strong measures should be taken against the smallest of offences, (5) ....
the offenders do not move on from petty to more serious crime.

One thing that all people agree on is that the fear of crime has a detrimental effect on
society and (6) .... communities should be helped to understand the real
threat of crime in their area. The old saying 'Prevention is better than cure' is still valid,
with a lot of local authorities setting up Crime Prevention Programmes for schools,
businesses and homeowners. In many cases, these help to reduce fear and also the
incidence of crime, (7) .... the clear information and practical suggestions
they provide.

Word-building: nouns

Complete the table with the noun form of the words in the box. Be careful with spelling.

detect   develop   discourage   identify   illegal   intend
invent   prevent   punish   secure   stupid   suspect

equipment	destruction	responsibility

Use of English

1 Read the text below. Use the word given in capitals at the end of each line to form a word that fits in the space in the same line. There is an example at the beginning **(0)**.

Kleptomania, which means a mania for stealing things, is a mental **(0)** .....*abnormality*..... **ABNORMAL**
which afflicts both young and old. It is different from **(1)** ...., as the **ROB**
culprit is often quite capable of paying for the things he or she takes. Some
kleptomaniacs steal things and then have no memory of the **(2)** .... **THIEVE**
afterwards. Having a **(3)** .... for stealing things can cause terrible **CONVICT**
damage to a person's future and also cause **(4)** .... to their family **EMBARRASS**
and friends. Sometimes psychiatric **(5)** .... cures it, but in general **TREAT**
there are no permanent **(6)** .... to the problem. Most victims **SOLVE**
complete therapy in the **(7)** .... that they will probably feel the **KNOW**
urge to steal things again. Those who succeed in defeating the illness completely are in
a **(8)** .... **MINOR**

2 Read the text below and decide which answer **A**, **B**, **C** or **D** best fits each space.

The young man had lived in a slum area of the city all his life and it was just a matter
of time before he was in **(1)** .... with the law. At school, which he hardly ever
attended, not only did he **(2)** .... the school property but he was also a bully,
frightening and beating up other children. When he was fifteen, he was **(3)** ....
for breaking into a local shop. At the age of sixteen, he was **(4)** .... with assault.
He got off with two years' **(5)** .... for this and was set free. Within six months, he
was back in **(6)** .... after he had been arrested for stealing cars. This time, he was
(7) .... to two years in prison. After his release, he again turned to crime. This
time it was bank robbery. At his trial he pleaded **(8)** ...., despite the fact he had
been caught red-handed. He was found **(9)** .... and the judge sentenced him to ten
years **(10)** .... Sociologists blame his background, while others say he was
just bad.

1	**A** problems	**B** defence	**C** trouble	**D** court
2	**A** mug	**B** vandalise	**C** thieve	**D** rob
3	**A** accused	**B** charged	**C** sentenced	**D** arrested
4	**A** charged	**B** accused	**C** released	**D** suspected
5	**A** punishment	**B** bail	**C** probation	**D** fine
6	**A** court	**B** probation	**C** jail	**D** trial
7	**A** punished	**B** accused	**C** committed	**D** sentenced
8	**A** guilty	**B** suspicion	**C** innocent	**D** free
9	**A** suspicious	**B** guilty	**C** illegal	**D** against
10	**A** prison	**B** probation	**C** offence	**D** imprisonment

Developing reading skills

Lead-in

1 Look at the pictures below and answer the following questions, using the phrases in the box.

   1 What has happened?

   2 What would need to be done to put the situation right?

   3 What public services would be involved and what would they need to do?

rescue stranded people	**try to control the flooding**
prevent the outbreak of fire	**set up emergency facilities**
search for survivors	**pump away water**
remove the damaged train	**offer support to victims**
take care of the injured	**assist the police**

2 Look at the following list of services that are available to the public. Which three would you like to see improved in your town or city? Give reasons for your answers.

- transport
- sports facilities
- help for homeless and underprivileged people
- hospitals and medical services
- schools and libraries
- Internet access
- phone and postal services
- recycling
- the emergency services
- museums and art galleries
- entertainment, e.g. cinema and theatre

Reading task: Multiple matching (questions)

Strategy: Recognising words which introduce examples

1 Scan through the following short texts and find the answers to the following questions. Choose from the services **A–C**.

Which service:

provides special equipment? **1** ☐

is endorsed by people in power? **2** ☐

can offer ongoing help after the service has been first used? **3** ☐

would expect you to return something to the person offering the service? **4** ☐ **5** ☐

tip

Look for words and phrases which introduce examples of items referred to in the questions. These include *for example, such as, namely, like, for instance, (ranging) from … to, include(s)*, etc.

A Service with a smile

Floral services exist in all parts of Britain. In most flower shops, skilled florists select and arrange flowers for occasions from birthdays to funerals. It is possible to send all kinds of flowers, including roses, daffodils and tulips, or more exotic varieties. Most florists have a telephone service, and with a simple call, they will organise for your flowers to meet their destination almost anywhere in the world under their next-day delivery service.

Bigger florists can also offer other services, such as deliveries of floral and plant displays to offices and even special deliveries to hospitals. Also available is advice and maintenance of plants, and even a rental service.

C The BBC World Service

The BBC World Service transmits radio programmes around the world in 45 languages from English to Arabic. It has a commitment to provide comprehensive, in-depth news and information to help meet worldwide needs for education and training. For example, there are programmes which can be used to help in the study of the English language, and to give people overseas access to British culture and entertainment. Among those who have expressed their thanks to the BBC are two European leaders, namely Lech Walesa of Poland and Václav Havel of the former Czechoslovakia.

2 Scan through the texts again and find the words and expressions that introduce examples.

3 Complete the following texts with words or expressions which introduce examples. Sometimes more than one answer is possible.

1 Our attendants are on hand while the pool is open. Their responsibilities .... life-saving and teaching young people how to swim.

2 Our travel office can provide you with information on holiday destinations all over the world. .... , if you like trekking, we can advise where to go, or if it's whitewater rafting you seek, then we can help you there too.

3 Our agents will do everything possible to help you find suitable accommodation. Prices vary greatly, and for better-equipped rooms, ... those with en-suite bathrooms and television facilities, expect to pay more.

B Biking around town

Local authorities are working hard to find ways to help locals and tourists make the most of Britain's cities, while protecting the environment. For instance, nowadays bicycle hire is available throughout the country. At the public's disposal there is a range of bikes, such as tandems, trikes, and 'harmonies' which can take three riders. In most cities, the cost for a day's hire ranges from £10 per day for a mountain bike to £20 a day for a tandem, complete with safety equipment. This includes a helmet, gloves, and a puncture repair kit.

Exam practice: Part 4

You are going to read some information about services which are provided to the public in Britain. For Questions **1–14**, choose from the services **(A–E)**. The services may be chosen more than once. When more than one answer is required, these may be given in any order. There is an example at the beginning **(0)**.

> **Remember!**
>
> Remember to look for words and expressions which introduce examples. You will also need to use other strategies.

Which service

stresses the choice of food available?   **0** **B**

does not refer to the past unfavourably?   **1** □   **2** □

returns customers' money if they are dissatisfied?   **3** □

compares itself unfavourably with other services?   **4** □

provides a service whereby customers can send messages?   **5** □

has staff that do more than one would expect?   **6** □

stresses the need for cooperation with other services?   **7** □

mentions how quickly it will reply to customers?   **8** □

stresses that its staff are knowledgeable about their jobs?   **9** □

would not take action if customers were unhappy with the service they received?   **10** □

charges extra for some of their services?   **11** □   **12** □

offers information in a range of formats?   **13** □

is obliged to be helpful by law?   **14** □

Services

A Coach services

A great favourite with students on limited budgets, coach services today are a far cry from their predecessors of some years ago. They are provided by a wide range of operators offering road transportation throughout the length and breadth of the country. Not to be outdone by the airlines, most coach terminals have comparable facilities such as check-in desks and exclusive lounges for the comfort of the traveller. Once on board, passengers can take advantage of services and facilities that include air-conditioning, a washroom, a TV, reclining seats, a choice of affordable light refreshments or even complimentary tea or coffee. Unlike planes and trains, however, the coach is at the mercy of road traffic and this can lead to delays and missed appointments. In order to offset this, refunds are promised to passengers when serious inconvenience occurs due to delays.

B Rail services

While the intercity rail services provide a fast non-stop service between major British cities, they can also be subject to major hold-ups, which is a source of great irritation to travellers. Attempts are being made to keep passengers informed of delays and problems, and to provide an improved service overall. Although in the past railway employees seemed to have little respect for passengers, today information is relayed over speakers in each carriage in a polite and pleasant voice. In keeping with the desire to improve services for passengers, all trains provide a trolley buffet service with a selection of refreshments and snacks brought directly to the passenger. Alternatively, hot meals and drinks can be obtained in the restaurant carriage. Unlike other public transportation systems, trains also have an informal lounge carriage where travellers can make use of modern communication systems. Passengers can link up to the Internet, for example, or use fax facilities if they wish, although this is in addition to the fare paid for the journey.

C Local services

The reception area of all local government offices in the United Kingdom is awash with leaflets and brochures detailing all the services provided by the local authority, including facilities and amenities provided by the local council. Information also relates to the various public works, which come under the umbrella of local town halls who are responsible for a host of diverse services such as refuse collection, street sweeping, road maintenance, car parks, street lighting, museums, libraries, school catering, leisure and community facilities. To do their job effectively and efficiently, councils must work closely with other local authorities and voluntary organisations. These usually include health, education and community services. For those who are dissatisfied with the standard of service received, a complaints procedure operates in all local councils. Investigations into the complaint are usually carried out within a week and a full response is sent soon after.

D Library services

Operated by highly-trained and efficient staff, libraries provide a wealth of information, from advice on health, to how to locate a particular piece of music. Apart from books, libraries also provide items like videos, CD-ROMs and music cassettes on loan to the public. Many libraries now enjoy the fruits of technology and members of the public can have access to computer terminals which are linked to the Internet. In line with recent legislation, librarians nowadays are duty-bound to provide a prompt, efficient and courteous service, which is a complete turnaround from years gone by. They are very helpful and will often go out of their way to provide whatever assistance is required.

E Careers centres

In the increasingly complex world of job hunting, careers centres all over England provide an invaluable service to school-leavers. They are open every day of the week except Bank Holidays, and can be of great use to young people who need information and help regarding their future. Friendly, cooperative staff will provide assistance with filling in application forms, for instance, and they can give advice and information on a range of issues associated with specific jobs, namely, what qualifications and/or skills are required, job conditions and rates of pay. In most centres, sympathetic staff will even make job enquiries on behalf of people who require further information about particular positions. In terms of other benefits, these centres also provide a range of facilities such as reference books, prospectuses, employer profiles and computerised information systems. Unlike other public offices, however, no complaints procedure exists for dissatisfied clientele.

Language development

Word attack

1 The compound nouns in the box are all taken from the texts on p.77. Complete the following sentences, using the nouns. Make any necessary changes.

> application form   complaints procedure
> computer terminal   fax facilities
> leisure facilities   local authority
> reference book   road maintenance

1 Many publications can be borrowed from the library, apart from .... which must not be removed.

2 Residents are worried about the number of car accidents in the area, so they want more money spent on ....

3 Some modern public buildings provide .... where people can find the information they require quickly, and also access the Internet.

4 I need to send and receive documents when I'm away from my office, so I always stay in a hotel with ....

5 The careers assistant helped me complete the .... for the post I was interested in.

6 If you are not satisfied with the service provided, please follow our

....

7 It is the duty of the .... to provide and maintain services for the inhabitants of a town.

8 I wish they would improve the .... in our town – there's nothing for teenagers to do at weekends.

2 Complete the following text, using the words in the box.

> access   agencies   commitment   excellence
> installation   leaflets   policy   politeness
> public   scheme

In recent years, the British government has set up a (1) .... to encourage civil servants to provide a better quality service to the (2) .... Each year, organisations receive an (3) .... award for providing the highest level of service. Their clients are impressed by the (4) .... of the staff and their (5) .... to ongoing customer care. This approach is consistent with the national (6) .... set down by the government and aims to measure the responses of all governmental (7) .... dealing with the public. In council offices, for example, automated queuing systems are now a regular feature. The (8) .... of such systems means a more efficient use of staff and shorter waiting times. In order to provide a comprehensive service for all members of the public, each government organisation is obliged to provide easy (9) .... to their premises for wheelchair-users. Information about the services provided is explained in (10) .... which are available at all public service offices.

Prepositional phrases

1 Look at the example from the text on p.77.

In terms of other benefits, …

2 There are other nouns that can be used to form prepositional phrases based on the pattern in **Exercise 1**. Complete the following sentences with *in*, the correct noun from the box and another preposition after the noun.

charge	common	honour	line	place
	response	time	touch	

1 After a long wait, the clerk finally got .... us about our complaint.

2 I arrived at the office .... my interview.

3 Whoever is .... the department is responsible for dealing with problems.

4 .... all other retired people, my grandparents receive a pension.

5 .... your query, we will be glad to send you the necessary information.

6 They installed a new word-processor .... the old typewriter.

7 .... new laws, all civil servants have to follow strict procedures.

8 The mayor made a speech .... the hard work of the emergency services.

Phrasal verbs

1 Look at the example from the text on p.77.

*Investigations into the complaint are usually **carried out** within a week …*

2 Complete the following sentences with the correct form of *carry* and the words in the box.

off	on	out	over	through

1 I tried to get the assistant's attention, but he just ignored me and .... talking to his colleague.

2 As soon as the water authority was informed about the flooding, they .... emergency repairs.

3 The urban development project has had many problems, but all the services involved are determined .... it .... to the end.

4 The role of head of customer services is a difficult one, but she .... it .... very well.

5 Despite many promises for improvement, the poor service that existed under the old management .... to the new one.

Use of English

Read the text below. Use the word given in capitals at the end of each line to form a word that fits in the space in the same line. There is an example at the beginning **(0)**.

My mother has just returned from a trip, full of praise for the travel company who organised it. The trip started off badly, due to my mother getting the travel times wrong, but the company managed to reorganise it for her. What impressed her most was the **(0)** ...*courtesy*... COURTEOUS
of the staff and in general the high quality **(1)** .... which was provided. SERVE

Although she had missed her connection, she was treated very **(2)** ...., SYMPATHY
told not to worry, before being allocated a new **(3)** .... time. While she DEPART
was waiting in the lounge, she was offered some light **(4)** .... which she REFRESH
gratefully accepted. She had never expected the staff of such a huge **(5)** .... ORGANISE
to show such pleasant **(6)** .... towards clients who were obviously in the BEHAVE
wrong. In fact, her needing to get a new ticket must surely have caused some **(7)** ...., CONVENIENT
but if so, she was not made aware of it.

In the past, if she had been late, she had found the **(8)** .... of other travel EMPLOY
companies to be rude and **(9)** .... In fact, it was precisely because of her HELP
(10) .... with them that she had changed her travel operator. SATISFY

Revision (Units 9–12)

1a Complete the table with the correct words from the box.

accuse agency apprehend bark breed chew coat commit customer getaway leaflet performance prompt quality release staff terrorist train vaccinate vet witness

Animals	Crime	Services

b Complete the following short texts with the words from **a**. Make any necessary changes.

1 While dogs make good pets, they need a lot of care and attention. Regardless of the (1) .... of dog you choose, they all need to be groomed regularly in order to keep their (2) .... looking shiny and healthy. Dogs will also require (3) .... against diseases and this means having to take your pet to the (4) .... on a regular basis. Having a dog also involves (5) .... it to behave well and not do things like (6) .... the furniture or people's shoes and slippers, or (7) .... at passers-by in the street.

2 Britain is no longer the land of slow shop assistants and endless queues. Many public places make every effort to provide a (1) .... service and efficient and friendly (2) .... Every bank, shop and supermarket is keen to convince the (3) .... that they are the best and that they offer the highest (4) .... They produce advertisements and publish (5) .... to highlight what is special about their organisation. This is also true of government (6) ...., who now publish annual targets and details of (7) .... in dealing with the public, budgets, and complaints.

3 Hardly a day goes by without television viewers (1) .... some sort of violence or crime being (2) .... on their screens. In fact, television is often (3) .... of influencing people to adopt criminal behaviour. I, however, find this hard to believe. In a recent film I saw, a group of (4) .... hijacked a plane and held the passengers at gunpoint for four days, before making their (5) .... in another plane. Of course, as always in films, the 'baddies' were later (6) .... by the hero of the film and the passengers were then (7) .... As television always shows the criminal getting caught in the end, I can't see how it would influence anyone to adopt a life of crime.

c Choose the best heading from the list (A–F) for each of the texts (1–3) in **b**.

A The price of quality

B Our four-legged friends

C TV creates crime

D TV and reality

E A good deal for the general public

F Services for pet owners

2 Read the text below. Use the word given in capitals at the end of each line to form a word that fits in the space in the same line. There is an example at the beginning **(0)**.

The creation of huge, impersonal cities is one of the prices of **(0)** .modernisation.. .	MODERN
One of the **(1)** .... features of urban development is the apparent isolation	CHARACTER
and **(2)** .... of people towards each other. In many large cities around the	FRIEND
world, neighbours are **(3)** .... of each other's needs and even existence.	IGNORE
This is often attributed to the pressures of everyday life, which in themselves cause	
(4) .... in most people and a longing for a better lifestyle.	SATISFY
However, the **(5)** .... of cities as places to live continues to grow, without	POPULAR
any **(6)** .... of the quality of life in them or any attempt to change. People	CONSIDER
often feel that family **(7)** .... suffer due to the lack of space and there is	RELATION
almost a feeling of **(8)** .... in the smallest houses and flats. Many teenagers	PRISON
have to endure the **(9)** .... of having to share a bedroom with their brother	CONVENIENT
or sister. Although this may not sound **(10)** .... in itself, most people now	REASON
recognise the importance of having your own space.	

3 Read the text below and decide which answer **A**, **B**, **C** or **D** best fits each space.

Anger, like the common cold, seems to be part and parcel of life. It arises in predictable situations, yet it always seems sudden and unexpected. In extreme cases, people **(1)** .... others in a completely unacceptable way. They say and do things to those around them that would get them **(2)** .... if done in public. They scream, insult, and sometimes even **(3)** .... injury. When the outburst is over, people who have lost their temper feel **(4)** .... and try to come up **(5)** .... some sort of excuse or apology. Some people even decide to **(6)** .... part in therapy sessions in organisations **(7)** .... by professionals in anger management.

Of course, not all anger is negative. There is a place for parental anger when **(8)** .... up children. As children **(9)** ...., they need to understand anger in themselves and others. Being told **(10)** .... by a parent is not necessarily a bad thing, provided its purpose is to educate. Children should learn to accept this and not go into a bad **(11)** .... or threaten to leave home just because they have been criticised.

Different people **(12)** .... with their anger in different ways, but no matter how well we can control this emotion, we must always bear in **(13)** .... that it is there. Most people **(14)** .... to recognise when anger is about to strike and, as a result, they are unable to **(15)** .... their outburst.

1	**A** behave	**B** treat	**C** act	**D** show
2	**A** accused	**B** charged	**C** arrested	**D** sentenced
3	**A** make	**B** do	**C** create	**D** cause
4	**A** innocent	**B** convicted	**C** guilty	**D** suspicious
5	**A** for	**B** to	**C** through	**D** with
6	**A** take	**B** have	**C** become	**D** get
7	**A** treated	**B** worked	**C** organised	**D** run
8	**A** taking	**B** bringing	**C** growing	**D** raising
9	**A** rear	**B** rise	**C** raise	**D** grow
10	**A** to	**B** out	**C** into	**D** off
11	**A** anger	**B** temperament	**C** mood	**D** behaviour
12	**A** manage	**B** organise	**C** deal	**D** cooperate
13	**A** the brain	**B** view	**C** account	**D** mind
14	**A** avoid	**B** regret	**C** fail	**D** ignore
15	**A** tame	**B** refuse	**C** deny	**D** prevent

Transport

Developing reading skills

Lead-in

1a Match the names of the forms of transport in the box with the pictures.

coach   ferry   hovercraft   monorail
motorbike   tram   helicopter   yacht

b Which of the means of transport in **a** can you see in the place where you live? Which ones have you yourself been on?

c Choose one means of transport that you have never used but which you would enjoy going on. Say why.

2 Make statements about different means of transport, choosing the correct information from the table.

e.g. *A motorbike is convenient to use, but it is noisy and it can be dangerous.*

	is fast	is slow
a plane	is convenient to use	limits you by its timetable and routes
a tram	is cheap to travel on	is noisy
a car	is cheap to run	creates pollution
a bus	is clean	is expensive to run
a motorbike	is safe	is expensive to use
	is quiet	can be dangerous

3 Match the beginnings of the newspaper headlines (1–5) with the correct endings (a–e).

1	Rough seas	**a**	bring trolleys to a standstill
2	Collision at sea with tanker	**b**	set by new intercity train
3	City-wide power failure	**c**	prevent hovercraft from operating
4	Speed record	**d**	causes train derailment
5	Object thrown onto track	**e**	sinks ferry

Reading task: Multiple matching (headings)

Strategy: Understanding figurative language

1a Read the following heading. Which word in the heading is used figuratively (in a way that is different from its usual meaning)?

New high-speed train shatters speed record

b What is the reason for saying ***shatters*** *speed record* instead of ***breaks*** *speed record* in the heading? Choose the correct answer.

1 to show surprise that old speed record could be broken

2 to show the new speed achieved is a lot higher than the old record

3 to show that trying to break the existing record was dangerous

2a Headings often contain phrasal verbs, which can also have figurative meanings. Which of the expressions below (1–3) could you use instead of *run into* in the following heading?

Electric cars *run into* legal obstacles

1 drive into

2 come up against

3 bump into

---

tip

Use the rest of the words in a heading to help you work out the meaning of a phrasal verb.

---

b What do the phrasal verbs in *italics* in the following headings mean?

1 Driver faces prison sentence after *running down* pedestrian

2 Critics *run down* new car

3 New tax will *put* hundreds of pounds *on* new cars

4 Council plans to *put* extra late-night buses *on*

3 Use the words in **bold** to help you work out the meanings of the figurative expressions in *italics*.

1 **New cruise ship is** *a floating hotel*

2 **Plans for new airport** *fail to get off the ground*

3 **Plans for underground line** *are in the pipeline*

4 **Private railway company finally** *runs out of steam*

5 **Cash shortage** *puts the brake on* **development of new vehicle**

4a Skim through the first paragraph of a text on traditional forms of transport. You will see that the heading is missing.

1

Horses pulling carriages were obviously capable of lower speeds than modern cars, many of which are capable of very fast speeds. Yet it has been calculated that people who travelled by horse and carriage in London had shorter journey times than those of today's highly-stressed motorists. Of course, horse-drawn transport had the advantage that horses didn't wait at red lights and they didn't get stuck in traffic jams. Nevertheless, it certainly makes you question what kind of progress we have made over a hundred years.

---

b Look back at the above paragraph and at the headings **A–E** below. Decide which of the headings best corresponds to the paragraph.

A No lights to hold them up

B Drivers under pressure

C Primitive and slow

D Quicker by miles than horses

E Impressive machines going nowhere

5a Skim through the next paragraph and choose the most suitable heading from the list **A–D**.

2

Tourists find it charming when they go to the Greek islands and see donkeys still in use. However, it would be a mistake to think that the donkey has only survived as a local means of transport because it is a tourist attraction. Even expensive modern vehicles like pick-ups and jeeps are impractical on the steep, narrow mountain tracks that donkeys go up and down with ease. Vehicles can be unreliable, too. They can break down in the middle of nowhere. As for the donkey, all it needs to go on working day after day is to be given regular breaks to munch its way through some grass or certain bushes that it is particularly fond of.

A Tourists fall in love with them

B They cost the earth and let you down

C They can't cope when it's uphill

D Budget-priced transport you can count on

b Underline the phrases in the paragraphs that helped you choose the correct heading for each one.

Exam practice: Part 1

You are going to read a text from an information leaflet about electric cars. Choose the most suitable heading from the list **A–I** for each part **(1–7)** of the text. There is one extra heading which you do not need to use. There is an example at the beginning **(0)**.

Remember!

Remember to look out for figurative language and phrasal verbs that you can connect to key phrases in the text. You will also need to use other strategies.

A   They can handle long journeys

B   Ideal for running about locally

C   EVs are a dream to drive

D   Why go electric?

E   Big companies add their weight, too

F   An important step forward

G   Not such a new idea

H   Drivers got fed up with them

I   Cars for enthusiasts

exam tip

Some headings may have more than one possible meaning. Consider alternative meanings of the headings before you match the headings to the paragraphs.

Electric vehicles

0 — G

Small electric-powered vehicles, or 'EVs', as their supporters often refer to them, are being talked about as the cars of the future. Many people probably think of them as a revolutionary concept. Yet the surprising truth is that electric cars first made their appearance as long ago as the 1830s.

1

Early petrol-powered cars were noisy and often broke down, while electric cars were more reliable and quieter. However, despite the fact that in 1900 an electric-powered car was driven 180 miles without its batteries having to be charged, it was the restricted range of the majority of electric cars which caused them to lose out to their petrol-powered rivals. Drivers quickly tired of cars that they could only drive for a few miles before they had to stop to charge their batteries. It was only in vehicles that were needed to pull huge weights, like trains and trams, that electric engines were deemed preferable.

2

Today the EV is starting to make a comeback. While just about every major car manufacturer has a prototype electric car, the great majority of EVs that are actually out on the streets are models built by tiny independent companies or conversions carried out by amateurs. Anyone wanting to convert their own car can visit a number of sites on the Internet to find out how to go about doing this.

3

A converted vehicle allows the driver to go between 25 and 50 miles on a charge. The exact range depends on the type of battery that you decide to install. Probably the best option is to use 8-volt batteries which result in a reasonably light, and therefore fairly quick vehicle, which can still go 40 miles before its batteries need recharging. This is perfectly adequate for the daily needs of the average driver. EVs are easy to drive in city traffic and when they are returned to the garage for the night, the driver simply plugs them into the mains to recharge for the following morning.

4

At present, many EV owners say they have to have a second, conventional car because their EVs are restricted to short distances. However, experimental electric-powered vehicles are breaking range records all the time. Recently, a specially-designed, light-bodied vehicle went an impressive 373 miles on a single charge. The secret of its success was its nickel-metal hydride batteries which, unfortunately, are extremely expensive at present and more than the average enthusiast can afford.

5

Many battery types and battery chemistries are being tested. Researchers have come up with a new type of lead-acid battery. It is being tried out in vehicles being driven on the streets of Seattle and so far the researchers have been very pleased with its performance. It looks like these batteries may be able to deliver a 50 per cent increase to a vehicle's range and, most importantly, shouldn't cost the earth if they go into production.

6

It is the common belief that electric vehicles are slow and boring to drive. The reality is quite different, however. Recently, the land speed record for an EV was broken when one reached 183 miles per hour, and this record will certainly go on being exceeded. The low centre of gravity achieved by placing the batteries down low in an electric car gives it tremendous cornering ability. Moreover, whereas petrol engines have to build up power, an electric engine delivers instantaneous power to the driver the moment it is turned on. Once motorists have got used to the smoothness of electrically-powered vehicles, they find petrol engines rough and jerky by comparison.

7

An internal combustion engine has about 6,000 moving parts. An electric engine, in contrast, has about 12, so car owners who switch over from petrol engines will find they have much lower maintenance bills. An electric engine in a car is expected to last about a million miles. Compare that with the average life expectancy of a petrol engine. Through the harmful gases pouring out of their exhausts, conventional car drivers are all contributing to the smog that hovers over modern cities. EV drivers, in contrast, drive around knowing that their vehicles are emitting no exhaust gases at all.

Language development

Word attack

1 Look back at the text on p.85. Find the words and expressions that mean the same as the following definitions.

1 completely new and different

....

2 to pass an electric current through something so that it stores electricity

....

3 the distance which a vehicle can travel without having to stop for fuel

....

4 to change something from one system or purpose to another ....

5 to put a piece of equipment somewhere and connect it so that it is ready to be used

....

6 the place you can connect something to a supply of electricity ....

7 how well a car or other machine works

....

8 to change completely from one thing to another ....

9 the act of keeping something in good condition ....

10 the pipes on cars or machines through which gas passes ....

2 Complete the following text using the words and expressions from **Exercise 1**. Make any necessary changes.

When I first met Robert, he told me proudly that not only did he do all his own car
(1) ...., but he had even
(2) .... an old van into a mobile home, which he was going to take his family to the south of France in that summer. Although the engine was old, it was a diesel vehicle and it should last for years. He said he had done some work on it and he was very satisfied with its (3) .... He had also (4) .... a TV and a fridge, so when they arrived at a campsite, they would only have to connect up to
(5) .... to enjoy all the comforts of home. To save space, he had even designed a (6) .... new type of folding table which he could use as a bed at night.

On the day that he and his family left for France, Robert was embarrassed when he couldn't get his 'mobile home' started because he hadn't (7) .... the battery. When, at last, he did get it started, they set off, with filthy blue smoke pouring out of the
(8) .... They never made it to France, because they broke down at the end of the road!

Phrasal verbs

The phrasal verbs in the box all come from the text on p.85. Complete the following text with the correct form of the verbs.

break down   build up   carry out
come up with   find out   go about
go on   turn on

Joanna and I were driving through quite a remote, mountainous area late at night when our car
(1) .... We had stopped for a short break and when I (2) ....
the ignition to start the car again, nothing happened. We opened up the bonnet and looked at the engine. Neither of us knows much about car mechanics, so we doubted if we would be able
(3) .... what was wrong.
Even if we could identify the problem, how were we going to (4) .... fixing it?
We obviously weren't going to be able
(5) .... an emergency repair in the dark. Then Joanna (6) .... a suggestion. She said that the battery was probably dead and we should try pushing the car to see if we could get it started. So we both pushed it down the slope and gradually it (7) ....
speed. Her suggestion worked and we got the engine going again. After that, we
(8) .... driving without stopping until we got to the next town.

Some uses of *break*

1 Look at the example from the text on p.85.

*... the land speed record for an EV **was broken** when ...*

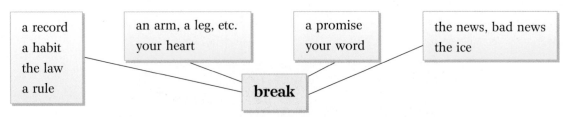

a record
a habit
the law
a rule

an arm, a leg, etc.
your heart

a promise
your word

the news, bad news
the ice

break

2 Complete the following sentences, using the correct form of *break* and appropriate expressions from the boxes. Make any necessary changes.

1 You ought to realise that you .... if you cycle at night without lights.

2 I was just getting off the bus when the driver suddenly started up again. I fell badly and I ...., just above the elbow.

3 The government is worried about congestion on the roads, so it is trying to get people to .... of driving to work every day.

4 It really .... when I looked at my brand new car and realised that it had scratches all over it.

5 Before he left that night, he told us he would drive carefully. After the accident, he admitted that he .... as soon as he got onto the motorway.

6 It was very hard .... to my father that his new car had been stolen.

7 We'd been sitting next to each other on the plane for hours without talking and it was only when we were coming in to land that we finally ....

8 The world air speed .... today by an experimental aircraft flying over the Pacific Ocean.

Use of English

Read the following text and decide which answer **A**, **B**, **C** or **D** best fits each space.

I was standing at the bus **(1)** .... in the pouring rain, waiting for a number 9 bus and it was late. The buses on this **(2)** .... are usually **(3)** .... time because they go through a suburban area where there is very little traffic to **(4)** .... them. I should know because I've been doing this same **(5)** .... to work every day for ten years. Anyway, when the bus finally arrived, you could see straightaway that the driver was very **(6)** .... because he was **(7)** .... late. I hardly had time to get **(8)** .... the bus before he started off again. The same thing happened when we stopped again to **(9)** .... a couple of passengers and to **(10)** .... some new passengers who were standing in the rain. He really was driving quite dangerously. Then it happened! He drove straight into a car. There was such a terrible bang that I felt sure it was a **(11)** .... accident. When I looked, I could see that the car was **(12)** .... but, fortunately, the driver and his passenger appeared to be unhurt.

1	**A** station	**B** terminus	**C** stop	**D** stage
2	**A** line	**B** route	**C** direction	**D** road
3	**A** in	**B** at	**C** to	**D** on
4	**A** delay	**B** hold	**C** slow	**D** keep
5	**A** journey	**B** trip	**C** travel	**D** tour
6	**A** nervous	**B** irritable	**C** excited	**D** unsteady
7	**A** going	**B** travelling	**C** running	**D** going
8	**A** in	**B** on	**C** into	**D** off
9	**A** set off	**B** put down	**C** put off	**D** set down
10	**A** fetch	**B** get up	**C** pick up	**D** take
11	**A** great	**B** serious	**C** heavy	**D** strong
12	**A** wrecked	**B** ruined	**C** destroyed	**D** spoilt

The environment

Developing reading skills

Lead-in

1 Look at the photograph and answer the questions.

1 What kind of things do people put in recycling bins?

2 Why do people use recycling bins?

3 Do recycling facilities like the ones in the photograph exist where you live? Do you use them? Why?/Why not?

2 Look at the following examples of environmentally-friendly activities. Say what benefits they provide, using the words in the box.

> **congestion   increase   oxygen   pesticides   pollution   reduce   sustain**

- recycling things like paper and plastic
- planting trees
- growing food organically
- using public transport rather than private cars

3 Make statements about environmental problems, choosing the correct information from the table.

e.g. *Acid rain is created by power stations and vehicle exhausts. It kills life in rivers and lakes.*

Environmental problems	Main causes	Most serious effects
water pollution	nuclear power stations	increases the risk of skin cancer
noise pollution	refrigerators, air-conditioning	leads to several forms of cancer
acid rain	forest fires and air pollution	creates floods and soil erosion
ozone layer damage	power stations, vehicle exhausts	threatens fish stocks
radiation	vehicles, loud music, power tools	results in breathing disorders
urban smog	oil, industrial waste, sewage	kills life in rivers and lakes
tree loss		damages people's mental health

4 Read the following statements by people about the places where they live. Say whether you think they are happy with their local environment, dissatisfied or concerned about it. Give reasons for your answers.

1 'This is a lovely place to live but if they build the new road through here, things will change. Instead of being able to hear birdsong we'll just get the roar of heavy traffic.'

2 'It would be so nice to have a few trees around us rather than concrete and rubbish everywhere you look.'

3 'There's a great view over the valley from the hill just up the road where I take the dog in the mornings.'

4 'This is a dirty old industrial area but we've got some nice parks and there are some pleasant walks down by the canal.'

Reading task: Multiple choice

Strategy: Identifying the writer's purpose

1 Skim through the following four texts and decide where each extract is from.

a a leaflet from an environmental organisation   **c** an advertisement for an adventure holiday

b an account of a journey through the rainforest   **d** a scientific discussion of an environmental issue

1

In parts of the forest, the vegetation is so dense that when you look up you can't even see the sky. The atmosphere is thick and heavy. You sweat all the time and you are constantly troubled by biting insects. The sounds of the rainforest are extraordinary: the songs of many different bird species, the cries of animals in the treetops that you never see. Underfoot, the ground is soft and your feet sink into the carpet of rotting leaves. You tread carefully, keeping an eye out for snakes that wind themselves around branches in your path.

3

The rate of deforestation worldwide is difficult to estimate. Recent studies have suggested that around 100,000 square kilometres are probably being lost annually. There are three identifiable consequences of forest loss to the global environment. The first is the contribution that the burning of trees makes to global warming through the release of carbon dioxide into the atmosphere. The second consequence is the loss of species brought about by the destruction of ecosystems. The third …

2

The rainforests contain about 50 per cent of all the plants and animals species on earth, and we haven't even identified most of them yet. The rainforests have already given us life-saving medical drugs and delights like oranges, lemons, bananas and chocolate. No one really knows what else lies waiting to be discovered. Yet, through our irresponsibility and greed, we are putting all such future discoveries at risk. The awful fact is that we are destroying about 50,000 plant and animal species a year through …

4

If you're expecting comfort and luxury, the Amazon is not the place for you. If you can put up with basic accommodation, biting mosquitoes, the sticky heat and frequent exhaustion, you may be the kind of person we're looking for. What you get in return for all this hardship is the chance to experience the most extraordinary place on earth: where you can see birds with the most exotic plumage imaginable, trees that reach the height of 20-storey buildings, …

2a Look at the table below and complete the first section, saying what the writer's purpose is in each of the texts 1–4. Put the number of the text in the correct column.

  b Complete the rest of the table by putting a tick (✓) in the appropriate boxes to identify features of the different styles of text. (Sometimes you will need to put more than one tick (✓) in a row.)

The writer's purpose	to analyse	to entertain	to warn	to challenge the reader
Text	3			
is written in a very formal style				
has words that express strong feelings				
contains facts intended to shock				
contains descriptive detail				
contains verbs in the passive voice				
addresses the reader directly				
contains the words *we* and *our*				
contains specialist vocabulary				

  c Answer the following questions.

    1 Why is one of the texts written in a very formal style?

    2 Why are words that express strong feelings used in one of the texts?

    3 What is the effect of using words like *we* and *our*?

    4 Why are descriptive details used a lot in one of the texts?

Exam practice: Part 2

You are going to read an extract from a book in which a famous conservationist and author describes his experiences of searching for rare animals in South America. For Questions **1–7**, choose the answer (**A**, **B**, **C** or **D**) which you think fits best according to the text.

Remember!

Remember to decide on the style of the text in questions which ask you about the writer's purpose. Ask yourself whether there is a lot of entertaining detail or if the writer is presenting factual information.

Most people seem to be under the impression that a frog is just a frog the world over. Nothing could be further from the truth, for with frogs and their near relatives, toads, you find that they vary from country to country, displaying a bewildering variety of shapes, sizes, colours, and habitats where they are to be found. The so-called flying frog of Asia, a large, tree-dwelling species, has developed very elongated fingers and toes. The skin between them is like a web and as this frog leaps from tree to tree, it spreads its fingers and toes wide so that it can glide like an aeroplane. The goliath frogs of West Africa measure two feet in length and can eat a rat, while a pygmy species of South America is about as big as your fingernail. In coloration, frogs are perhaps the only species that could seriously claim to rival birds, for there are frogs coloured red, green, gold, and blue. When it comes to rearing their young, frogs produce some startling results. The midwife toad of Europe hands her eggs over to the male who, in order to protect them, winds them around his hind legs and carries them around until they hatch. A species of tree frog glues two leaves together, and when water collects in the cup thus formed, the frog lays its eggs in this home-made pond.

Guiana has more than her fair share of frogs that possess ingenious methods of safeguarding their eggs and young, and the creek lands proved to be the best place for catching them. Bob was amusing himself by dragging one of these narrow, smelly little streams with a long-handled net, while I prowled hopefully around some tree roots. With the aid of a torch I succeeded in capturing three large tree frogs with huge eyes.

Bob continued doggedly with his net. I saw him haul his net out, as usual full of a pile of dirty leaves, and tip them out onto the bank. He was just going to plunge his net back into the water again when he stopped and peered down at the pile of leaves he had just pulled up.

Then he dropped the net and let out a delighted shout.

'I've got one!' he yelled.

'What have you got?'

'A pipa toad.'

'Nonsense,' I said.

'Come and have a look, then,' said Bob, bursting with pride.

He opened his hand for my inspection and revealed a strange, ugly creature. It looked, to be quite frank, like a brown toad that had been run over by a heavy truck. Its short, rather thin arms and legs stuck out stiffly, one at each corner of its squarish body, and it looked quite dead. It was, as Bob said, a large male pipa toad, perhaps one of the most curious amphibians in the world. Ever since we arrived in Guiana we had been trying to get specimens of this creature. Now, after Bob's success, we searched every inch of that small stream, producing a mountain of rotting leaves which we picked over as carefully as a couple of monkeys searching each other's fur. An hour later we had captured four more of these weird toads. Moreover one of them was a female with eggs, a prize that was worth anything in our eyes, for the breeding habits of the pipa toad are the most extraordinary thing about it.

At the beginning of the breeding season, the skin on the female's back becomes soft and spongy. When her eggs are laid they are deposited with the help of the male along her back, where they stick like glue. After they have been fertilised they sink into her skin, forming cup-like depressions. The soft tops of the eggs then harden, forming little pockets on her back. In these pockets her young spend the whole of their early life until they have fully developed when they push the little lid on the top of the pocket and make their way out into the dangerous world.

The female we captured could only just have had her eggs installed, for their lids were still soft. When her young were at last old enough to leave their mother's back they chose a moment when I was looking after their mother and the other animals I had collected on board a ship, in the middle of the Atlantic Ocean.

1 What is the purpose of the first paragraph?

   A to provide a scientific description

   B to show that frogs have similarities with birds

   C to emphasise variety in nature

   D to entertain readers

2 The writer and his assistant searched for frogs in Guiana because

   A the frogs in Guiana have wonderful colours.

   B the behaviour of Guianan frogs is interesting.

   C Guianan frogs are unusual in their appearance.

   D the frogs in Guiana live in unusual places.

3 The place where they searched for frogs was

   A dangerous.

   B unpleasant.

   C attractive.

   D uninteresting.

4 Bob

   A nearly missed a valuable find.

   B was systematic in his method of searching.

   C was about to give up when he found the toad.

   D was disappointed when he saw what his toad looked like.

5 The author particularly wanted to catch a pipa toad because

   A it is such an unusual-looking creature.

   B it is very difficult to find.

   C it is unique because it looks dead when alive.

   D it has a fascinating breeding method.

6 The female toad's babies

   A were born in dangerous circumstances.

   B were born soon after the author caught her.

   C were born at an inconvenient time.

   D were born in an unusual way for this species.

7 The writer's overall purpose in the text is to

   A inform his readers about a rare species.

   B make his readers like frogs and toads.

   C amuse his readers with a funny story.

   D interest his readers in the natural world.

exam tip

Texts that are written to entertain are often in a less formal style, with interesting, amusing and descriptive detail. Texts that are written to inform, warn or analyse are often in more formal style, with factual information and statistics.

Language development

Word attack

1 Look back at the text on p.90. Complete the following list of words, all of which are used in the text to describe how animals reproduce and take care of their young. All the words can be found in paragraphs 1 and 5. The first letter of each word is provided.

1 *rearing*................................

2 h................................

3 p................................

4 l................................

5 b................................

6 d................................

7 f................................

8 d................................

2 Complete the following sentences using the words from **Exercise 1**. Make any necessary changes.

1 A chicken can .... many eggs in a single week.

2 Birds' eggs require the warmth from the bodies of the parent birds in order ....

3 The baby bird slowly .... inside the egg.

4 Female fish release their eggs into the water, where the eggs .... by the male fish.

5 Many mammals like apes and monkeys are very good parents. They put a lot of effort into .... their young.

6 Some insects have a special tool with which they .... their eggs on the undersides of leaves.

7 The patterns and colours of birds' eggs make them hard to see and help .... them from predators.

8 Many zoos have tried to get pandas ...., so that the pandas born in the zoos can be returned to the wild.

3 Look back at the text on p.90. Find the words that mean the same as the following definitions.

1 the natural home of a plant or animal ....

2 a group of plants or animals of the same kind ....

3 moved around quietly, trying not to be seen ....

4 catching an animal after chasing or following it ....

5 animals that are able to live both on land and in water ....

6 single plants or animals that are typical of their kind ....

7 the hair that grows thickly over the bodies of some types of animal ....

8 unusual or surprising ....

4 Complete the following text, using the words from **Exercise 3**. Make any necessary changes.

Africa has some of the most interesting animal (1) .... in the world. The large mammals, like lions and elephants are well known, but there is also an extraordinary variety of birds, snakes, (2) .... and some of the (3) .... insects on earth.

In the old days, Europeans used to go to Africa to shoot magnificent (4) .... of lions and other large animals. A lot of animals were also killed to supply the (5) .... trade. Nowadays, however, visitors from Europe go to enjoy seeing the animals in their natural (6) .... There is simply no comparison between seeing a lion in a zoo and seeing one (7) .... at dusk, looking for an opportunity to hunt. Some of the national parks have too many lions and so some (8) .... and transferred to areas where the lion populations are smaller.

Raise, rise, rear, lay, lie

1 Look at the examples from the text on p.90.

*When it comes to **rearing** their young, …*

*… **lays** its eggs in …*

2 Complete the following sentences, using the correct form of *raise, rise, rear, lay* or *lie*.

1 Public concern about environmental issues .... considerably in recent years.

2 We came across a magnificent lion .... down in the shade of a tree.

3 We got some wonderful photos of a tiger cub .... its head on its mother's side.

4 In some parts of England, birds .... to be shot for sport during the shooting season.

5 In zoos, it can sometimes be difficult to get animals .... their young as they would do in the wild.

Compound adjectives

1 Look at the example from the text on p.90.

*… in this **home**-made pond.*

2 Complete the following newspaper article, using the compound adjectives in the box.

deep-sea   free-range   lead-free   man-eating   nuclear-free   world-famous

Environmentalists meeting at a conference in London today discussed several serious issues. A (1) .... conservationist expressed concern about the number of tigers still surviving in the wild. He suggested that one reason for the continuing decline in their numbers is the myth of the (2) .... tiger, which continues in some places, leading to tigers being shot by local farmers out of fear.

The conference delegates were warned that marine pollution appears to be getting worse, so much so that (3) .... fishing vessels are finding that their catches are decreasing every year.

Despite these ongoing problems, there are also some encouraging developments. In many countries, the demand for factory-farmed produce is falling, while there is increased demand for produce like (4) .... eggs and organically-grown vegetables.

Further good news for the environment is that more countries have declared themselves to be (5) .... zones and there has been a huge rise in the amount of (6) .... petrol being sold.

People and relationships

Developing reading skills

Lead-in

1a Look at the three photographs of different people. What do you notice about them first?

b What impressions do you get of each person in **a**? Talk about their appearance, mood and character, using the words in the box.

> arrogant   bored   casual   delighted   excited   glamorous   proud
> serious   smart   surprised   traditional   tribal   unsure   worried

2 Write the words in the box in the correct category in the table.

> annoyed   bald   beard   curly   depressed   dyed   elderly   excited   fed up
> freckles   fringe   getting on   middle-aged   moustache   overweight   plump
> slender   teens   well-built   wrinkles

Age	Hair	Build	Face	Attitude

Reading task: Gapped text

Strategy: Understanding connectors which give additional information

1 Skim through the descriptions (1–3) below and match each one to its possible source (a–d). There is one source too many. (Do not focus on the gaps in the three texts at this stage.)

a a biography

b a character reference for a job

c a personal letter

d an article from an educational magazine

1

The photo below shows a member of a group of peoples from Natal, South Africa, known collectively as Zulus. She is tall and well-built with the facial features which are typical of her people. [X] *Also*, she has got plaited hair which is surrounded by a beaded headband. Her clothing is a cylindrical garment of tightly-rolled cloth, covered in a sheath of beads in regional colours with typical female geometrical symbols. The males also have similar symbols on their clothing.

2

Angela Davies is still only in her early twenties and she is already a very competent and talented person. She is well-organised, conscientious and caring. She is also open to new ideas and willing to learn new techniques. [Y] When she gives you her word, you know you can depend on her.

3

I ended up sharing a room with Deborah. She is one of the most attractive but depressing people I know. She's tallish and quite slim with almost perfect skin and long blonde hair. Despite her looks, she's not exactly very pleasant company. [Z] *What's more,* she always expects the worst, and her reaction to every suggestion is 'What's the point?' In fact, she is really rather dull and has no sense of humour.

2 Read the texts again more slowly. Choose from the sentences **A–D** the one which best fits each gap (**X**, **Y** and **Z**), using the words in *italics* to help you. There is one extra sentence which you do not need to use.

A *Another thing* I like about her is that she loves to chat and gossip and is one of those people who talk quickly without seeming to take a breath.

B Her attitude is so negative and pessimistic that she pulls everyone down with her.

C *Further* important qualities she possesses are reliability and trustworthiness.

D Her earrings are made of metal and the teeth of wild animals.

Exam practice: Part 3

You are going to read an article about Australian Aborigines. Eight sentences have been removed from the article. Choose from the sentences **A–I** the one which fits each gap **(1–7)**. There is one extra sentence which you do not need to use. There is an example at the beginning **(0)**.

> **Remember!**
>
> Remember to look for connectors which introduce additional information. You will also need to use other strategies.

Australian Aborigines

Aborigines are the indigenous peoples of Australia. They were wandering hunters and food gatherers, without settled communities or knowledge of agriculture. Today these travelling tribes make up just over 1.5 per cent of the country's population of 18 million. Aboriginal people have been present in Australia for thousands of years, but a lack of definitive archaeological evidence means that accounts vary as to exactly how long. Some estimate that Aborigines have been in the country as far back as 60,000 years ago. **0** **H**

Vital to the task of piecing together the history of the Aborigines are the tools that have survived from the earliest periods. The stone tools that have been found indicate little change throughout the Pleistocene periods (from 1.65 million years ago until 10,000 years ago), and it is now known that it was not until around 6,000 years ago that there was a radical development in the implements themselves, with small, delicately-worked points and blades being produced. **1** Examples of wooden tools rarely survive, though one unique archaeological find proved that the boomerang, used chiefly as a weapon and for sport, together with the barbed spear were invented more than 10,000 years ago.

2 Aboriginal painters used charcoal for black and pipe clay for white. Blues and greens have been added to the palette only in recent times. Painting techniques involve various methods of applying the paint, including spraying it from the mouth, painting it on with a brush formed from the chewed end of a twig, or a finger, or splashing it on with grass. Much of the work, which is sold for large sums of money today, contains colourful images of the varied wildlife of the country.

3 Identifying the species, however, is rarely possible because of problems in scale. Hunters may be shown with bundles of pointed spears, or spears may be travelling through the air, or stuck in the prey with a spurt of blood. Boomerangs and nets may also be shown in use, and scenes may include a group of people driving animals towards a trap or stalking them from hides. **4**

Other aspects of Aboriginal life revealed in art include information relating to normal everyday items such as knives and dishes, plants that were gathered, clothing, together with some features of ceremonial life like costumes and dancing figures. In some scenes, there is clear evidence of their tribal customs. One of the many of these strange customs rigidly observed by the Aborigine is the avoidance of the mother-in-law. **5**

Aborigines are a particularly moral race and the laws are strictly enforced, especially those governing family and marriage. In the past, breaches of certain laws were sometimes punishable by death.

6 The act of painting is itself religious, and may be accompanied by singing, or may be part of a wider ceremony.

Additionally, art also played a role in aspects of land ownership and the recording of stories. The right to paint particular motifs, and in particular sites, was restricted to ownership of stories, and required seniority in a clan. **7**

Life for women was by no means easy among these nomads. Besides having to deal with the family, they were responsible for carrying heavy loads of household equipment, spare weapons and so on, whenever they moved from one place to another. The male's main task was to provide the food for his family.

A Many of their myths and legendary tales are as imaginative as those of much more technologically-advanced peoples.

B There was even a gender restriction both in depiction, as some sites were painted only by women, and in who was permitted to see particular sites.

C Another crucial form of archaeological evidence is Aboriginal art.

D As these were more complex choppers and scrapers, used mainly to create other tools of wood, this was a great step forward.

E Under dire penalty, no man may look at his wife's mother, nor may she look upon him.

F As with most of the world's native tribes, religious life is clearly a major feature in Aboriginal culture, as we see with the discovery of paintings of dreaming figures of all kinds, along with mystical symbols whose meaning is not fully understood

G As well as figures depicted with weapons, actual weapons such as boomerangs and axes were also stencilled on to rocks, giving an exact outline of the implement concerned.

H During this time, there has been a great change in the geography of Australia, as it has evolved from being mostly green and lush to its present state of mainly desert, and this has brought about the decline in the native population.

I Hunting scenes depicted in their art usually involve kangaroos and wallabies or emus.

Language development

Word attack

The words in the box are taken from the text on p.96. Complete the following text, using the words.

> **archaeological   colourful   earliest   household**
> **indigenous   tribal   varied   wandering**

Recent discoveries of (1) .... evidence from the (2) ....
periods of human existence show that (3) .... groups have existed
on earth for much longer than was previously thought. The (4) ....
peoples of North America, for instance, are now known to have been groups of
(5) .... tribes who crossed the Bering Straits from Asia before finally
developing permanent settlements in their new land. They brought with them on their
journey all kinds of (6) .... equipment, and weapons such as knives
and spears. Additionally, they brought with them their sacred customs and rituals.
America at that time had a rich and (7) .... wildlife which supported
the new peoples. Evidence of their prosperity is seen in the (8) ....
paintings and images which exist on the walls of caves found near where they lived.

Expressing negatives

Complete the following sentences using the words and expressions in the box.

> **a lack of   rarely   little   by no means   not until**

1 After the flooding of the area, it is .... strange that little evidence of
   the indigenous people remains.
2 Finding examples of wooden tools intact is .... possible.
3 Due to .... evidence, it is hard to determine dates.
4 There has been .... change in their painting techniques over the
   centuries.
5 It was .... the Europeans arrived in Australia that the decline of the
   Aborigines started.

Compound adjectives

1 Put a tick (✓) in the boxes to form a compound adjective.

	headed	skinned	dressed	minded	hearted	behaved	tempered
strong-							
well-							
quick-							
light-							
cold-							
half-							
open-							

2 Complete the following sentences, using the compound adjectives from **Exercise 1**.

1 The children sat quietly during the train journey. They were very ....

2 She always gets angry so easily. In fact, she's the most .... person I know.

3 Andrew wasn't very enthusiastic about the suggestion, but he finally agreed in a .... manner.

4 Being .... is important when trying to create a good impression at public functions.

5 Try to be .... about the issue and do not let your feelings influence your decision.

Use of English

Read the following text and decide which answer **A**, **B**, **C** or **D** best fits each space.

My grandfather was a very **(1)** .... man with distinctive **(2)** .... He had thick black hair and a **(3)** .... trimmed moustache. Although he wasn't very tall, he was **(4)** .... with strong shoulders and muscular arms. He was always very well-dressed and took great pride in his **(5)** .... He was so **(6)** .... of the way he dressed that his brothers used to make fun of him. This didn't upset him as he had a good **(7)** .... of humour. In fact, he had such a great **(8)** .... that everyone loved him.

1	**A** pretty	**B** lovely	**C** sweet	**D** handsome
2	**A** characters	**B** humour	**C** features	**D** personalities
3	**A** clearly	**B** neatly	**C** smartly	**D** gracefully
4	**A** well-made	**B** well-formed	**C** well-behaved	**D** well-built
5	**A** appearance	**B** presence	**C** look	**D** outfit
6	**A** conscientious	**B** conscious	**C** considerate	**D** unconscious
7	**A** feeling	**B** awareness	**C** sensation	**D** sense
8	**A** personality	**B** feature	**C** mood	**D** temper

Developing reading skills

Lead-in

1 Match the following statements to the places on the map.

   1 It would be wonderful to do a tour of the capital city.

   2 The loch would be great for fishing and we could try to spot the monster!

   3 I would love to see all the ancient sites.

   4 We could visit the architect's unfinished masterpiece.

   5 We could visit the places where *Schindler's List* was filmed.

   6 We could have a go at snowboarding.

2 What are the attractions or disadvantages of the following types of holiday?

   • sightseeing in a modern city

   • skiing

   • a tour of major capital cities

   • a visit to ancient sites

   • a beach holiday

   • an activity holiday, e.g. diving, whitewater rafting

3 What places in your country would you recommend to visitors?

Reading task: Multiple matching (questions)

Strategy: Understanding words and expressions which show an opinion or attitude

> **tip**
>
> It's important to understand words and expressions which show a writer's opinion or attitude. These are often linked to functions like advising, recommending, reminding, etc. For example, the sentence *The city is worth seeing* means the writer is recommending the city.

1 Scan through the following extract from a travel brochure and match the phrases in *italics* to the following functions.

  1 advising **4** suggesting

  2 promising **5** preferring

  3 offering

Tired of the same old kind of holiday, then *why not try* Zita Tours?

Packed into our latest brochure are over 100 tour ideas and itineraries, visiting more than 35 destinations throughout Britain and Europe. As an added bonus, a host of sightseeing and excursion opportunities are included to ensure a memorable holiday. Booking is easy; just pick up the phone and *let us help* you plan a trip to an exotic location or to exciting cities like Rome or Madrid. If foreign travel is out, then take to the English countryside where *you will certainly discover* an unbelievable variety of places to visit. Along every route, picturesque villages teem with tourists from all over the world. Lying at the heart of one of the most scenic stretches of countryside in England and surrounded by unspoilt beauty is Tunbridge Wells, the ideal location for a short break or tour of the Kentish countryside. *If you would rather escape* from it all to somewhere less crowded and peaceful, just browse through our wide selection of brochures and our expert staff will be glad to provide assistance.

> Remember our package deals are very popular, so *it's wise to book early to avoid disappointment.* Why not call us right now?

---

2 Match the statements (1–5) with the functions (a–e).

  1 'I'd sooner visit somewhere warm and sunny this summer.'

  2 'There's a danger of tropical storms in the Caribbean, so I think you should reconsider your destination.'

  3 'There's a chance that it will rain there, so take an umbrella.'

  4 'These snapshots remind me of my first time in Madrid.'

  5 'Don't forget to buy lots of souvenirs when you are there.'

  a making a suggestion

  b stating a preference

  c talking about an experience

  d reminding someone to do something

  e saying something is possible

Exam practice: Part 4

You are going to read a magazine article about five people's opinions of five different cities in the world. For Questions **1–16**, choose from the people **(A–E)**. Some of the people may be chosen more than once. When more than one answer is required, these may be given in any order. There is an example at the beginning **(0)**.

Remember!

Remember to look for words and expressions which show a writer's opinion or attitude. You will also need to use other strategies.

Which writer

is sorry that more people do not visit the city?	0 A
advises visitors to make travel arrangements in advance?	1 / 2
says that visitors will regret not being able to see everything they want to?	3
says the city has had an unfortunate recent history?	4
stresses the natural beauty of the setting?	5 / 6
admits that the city has problems?	7
says he/she would like to make the city their permanent home?	8
mentions how best to get around the city?	9
urges visitors not to miss a particular sight?	10
is confident that people who visit the city will share his/her feelings?	11
promises good weather?	12 / 13
mentions a legend?	14
recommends the local food?	15
suggests travelling outside the city as well as inside?	16

**Steven Taylor asked five of our readers to talk about their favourite cities.
Here is what they had to say.**

A George, Athens

The majority of annual visitors to Greece arrive on package tours to the Greek islands and rarely get the opportunity to explore the sights of Athens, which is a pity, because despite the noise and traffic jams, it is one of the most exciting and fascinating cities in Europe. To make sure you get to see the most important sights, you can book a city tour at a very reasonable price. However, it is always wise to pre-book tours of Athens, especially if you are going to come in August. There is a wealth of scenery to enjoy in the surrounding countryside, too, so try to take in other one-day excursions out of the city. At the heart of the city, nestled at the foot of the Acropolis is Plaka, the oldest and most picturesque neighbourhood in Athens. Overlooked by the glorious temple of the Parthenon, it is a maze of narrow streets running in all directions around the Acropolis.

B Richard, Rio de Janeiro

If I had the choice of any city in the world in which to live, it would be Rio. It is one of the most romantic cities in the world, blessed with a wonderful sunny climate you can count on and a breathtaking coastline. Rio is undoubtedly one of those favoured places in the world, whose names have a universal romantic appeal. The effect Rio has on the visitor is unforgettable. It is set in a stunning location surrounded by lush green vegetation and the sea. Central Rio lies on the western shore of the bay, with world-famous Sugar Loaf Mountain standing guard to the natural harbour, while to the west is Copacabana, that stretch of brilliant white sandy beach that to the locals is without equal. A blend of European and South American culture, Rio is the highlight of any visit to Brazil.

C John, Venice

Italian cities are famed for their history and culture but to many people Venice is unquestionably one of the finest cities in the world. Constructed on an archipelago of 18 small islands separated by a dense network of waterways, Venice is geared to accommodating the millions of tourists who flock here annually. Known locally as 'The Queen of the Adriatic', Venice is best seen by water. Relax as you wind your way along the Grand Canal past incredible facades of Gothic and Renaissance palaces and magnificent churches below the elegant Rialto Bridge. Go sightseeing around the numerous palaces and take in the wonderful architectural heritage. Venice today still looks much as it did in the 13th century, with the exception of a few transformations to some buildings. Crowded throughout the summer months, reasonably-priced accommodation is almost impossible to find, so an advance booking is essential.

D Emma, Barcelona

The weather can make or break a holiday but in the Catalonian capital in the summer months, rest assured that the sun will shine each day. I can't imagine anyone not loving Barcelona. It is a stylish, cosmopolitan city with the romantic Mediterranean on its doorstep. Visitors should take every opportunity to sample the wonderful cuisine as well as the famous Catalonian hospitality, (and will no doubt wish they had more time to explore the city). Despite the rapidly-changing skyline of the modern city, which reflects the present age, it remains an enchanting place. For the culturally-minded, there are a great many museums, custodians of a unique historical and cultural heritage. Among the most popular with an international reputation is the Picasso Museum, which houses many of the painter's works and hosts many temporary exhibitions.

E Anna, Warsaw

Warsaw is a city steeped in history. Situated on the banks of the Vistula river, Warsaw gets its name from Wars, a fisherman and, Sava, a mermaid he had rescued. Fortunately, despite its almost total destruction in the early forties, Warsaw is teeming with places of interest. The Old City, which has been restored, centres on the medieval market square near the river and is surrounded by Renaissance and Baroque houses. A must for all visitors is the Palace of Culture and Science, which affords a panoramic view of the entire city. Also well worth visiting in Lazienki Park is The Palace on Water, built in the 18th century as the summer palace of Stanislas II Augustus, the last king of Poland.

Language development

Word attack

1 Match the words (1–6 and a–f) to form sets of words that often together.

1	traffic	**a**	tour
2	package	**b**	view
3	panoramic	**c**	price
4	international	**d**	heritage
5	cultural	**e**	jam
6	reasonable	**f**	reputation

2 Complete the following sentences with the words from **Exercise 1**. Make any necessary changes.

1 Many tourists nowadays prefer to go on
.... where
everything has been arranged for them.

2 We were hoping to see as much of the area as
possible, but we ended up sitting in
.... behind
long queues of other tourists.

3 It was well worth making the effort to get to
the top of the mountain, as we had a
magnificent ....
of the whole area.

4 The many galleries in Madrid has given the city
an .... for art.

5 Many countries promote their strong
.... to attract tourists.

6 The travel agent assured us that local
souvenirs could be bought at a
...., but in
the end they cost us a fortune.

Word-building: prefixes

1 Match the meanings of the prefixes highlighted in the words (1–5) in **bold** to the meanings (a–e).

1	**trans**atlantic	**a**	more than necessary, available, etc.
2	**over**booked	**b**	across
3	**pre**arranged	**c**	again
4	**post**-war	**d**	before
5	**re**visit	**e**	after

2 Complete the table below with suitable words for each category.

transatlantic	**over**booked	**pre**arranged	**post**-war	**re**visit

Passive voice + prepositions

Complete the text on p.105 with the correct form of *be* where necessary and the expressions in the box. There is one extra expression which you do not need to use.

> **blessed with   crowded throughout   famed for   geared to   lined with
> located near   set in   situated on   surrounded by**

(1) .... the banks of the river Seine, Paris (2) ....
its magnificent architecture and buildings. Perhaps the most famous of all Parisian
constructions is the Eiffel Tower, built in 1889 and (3) .... the beautiful
park of the Champ de Mars. The city (4) .... numerous Gothic
cathedrals and churches.

(5) .... the year, Paris is a cosmopolitan melting pot of people from all
over the world. Life in Paris (6) .... accommodating the millions of
tourists who visit it each year. Along the narrow streets of Montmartre, (7) ....
clubs and bars, the visitor can experience the exciting nightlife Paris offers. In the centre of
the city lies the Île de la Cité which (8) .... the waters of the Seine and
on which stands Notre Dame Cathedral.

Use of English

1 Complete the second sentence so that it has a similar meaning to the first, using the word
given. **Do not change the word given**. You must use between two and five words,
including the word given.

1 I would like to visit Los Angeles one day.   **wish**

I .... Los Angeles one day.

2 I don't want to go on a package tour.   **rather**

I .... on a package tour.

3 'Don't forget to buy some souvenirs, Simon,' said Kostas.   **reminded**

Kostas .... some souvenirs.

4 'It would be wise to pre-book your flight,' said Michael.   **advised**

Michael .... my flight.

5 I will never forget my first impression of Cracow.   **remember**

I will .... my first impression of Cracow.

2 Read the following text and decide which answer **A**, **B**, **C** or **D** best fits each space.

When travelling **(1)** ...., it is always worth taking the time to do some **(2)** ....
and find out about the culture of the place you are visiting. One of the best ways to
choose what to see is to get a **(3)** .... which has details about all the different cultural
(4) .... on offer. Of course, if you are on a package tour, your tour operators will
normally provide you with an **(5)** .... of the places you will see. They take
responsibility for **(6)** .... the travel arrangements. This helps to make your
(7) .... more enjoyable, as you do not need to worry about finding out where to go.
From the moment you **(8)** .... until the time of departure, everything is taken care of,
from booking flights to **(9)** .... visits to places of interest. With a package tour, all your
holiday needs will have been taken care of and everything will have been **(10)** ....
months in advance. You never need to worry about your hotel being **(11)** .... as your
agent will have checked and **(12)** .... all the travel arrangements.

1	**A** foreign	**B** internationally	**C** overland	**D** abroad
2	**A** sights	**B** sightseeing	**C** history	**D** viewing
3	**A** prospectus	**B** leaflet	**C** guide	**D** brochure
4	**A** customs	**B** sites	**C** museums	**D** destinations
5	**A** agenda	**B** article	**C** identification	**D** itinerary
6	**A** booking	**B** making	**C** taking	**D** having
7	**A** voyage	**B** flight	**C** cruise	**D** trip
8	**A** arrive	**B** reach	**C** come	**D** go
9	**A** organising	**B** making	**C** taking	**D** doing
10	**A** previewed	**B** pre-set	**C** prescribed	**D** prearranged
11	**A** pre-booked	**B** overcharged	**C** overloaded	**D** overbooked
12	**A** unchecked	**B** rechecked	**C** reused	**D** post-checked

Revision (Units 13–16)

1a Complete the table with the correct words from the box. Some words can fit in more than one category.

> competent   conservationist   custom   deforestation   delay   determined
> distance   erosion   generation   habitat   identity   inhabit   itinerary   marine
> pesticide   route   settlement   species   traffic jam   trip   vehicle

Transport and travel	The environment	People and characteristics

b Complete the following short texts with the words from **a**. Make any necessary changes.

1 As motorway networks improve throughout Europe, travelling long (1) .... by road is no longer the problem it was years ago. Each year, huge numbers of people set off in their own (2) .... on their annual holiday. They believe that having their own means of transport will enable them to choose their own (3) .... for their holiday. Independent travel also allows people to change their (4) .... to include places that the majority of tourists never get to see. However, international travel is not the same as having a day out or going on a family (5) .... to the seaside. As most Europeans tend to take their holidays at the same time of year, huge (6) .... occur on the roads of Europe as people head for the most popular resorts. Such congestion causes (7) .... in getting to destinations and makes for an unhappy start to a holiday. Perhaps package holidays are a better bet after all.

2 Despite the efforts of Friends of the Earth and other (1) ...., humans continue to destroy the (2) .... of huge numbers of different (3) .... of animals and plants each year. Modern farming techniques cause great destruction and the widespread use of (4) .... means that rivers become polluted. This, in turn, affects (5) .... life when the toxic substances enter the sea. In the huge rainforests of South America, (6) .... ravages the homes of the wildlife of the region. Without the trees to keep the soil in check, there are serious problems with (7) .... which results in mud slides during heavy rains.

3 The Inuit, better known to most as Eskimos, (1) .... the Arctic coasts of North America and Canada. Today, scattered around the shores of Hudson Bay are tiny (2) .... of Inuit, whose lives and traditional (3) .... are under threat from the modern world. Despite the invasion of technology into their world, the Inuit are (4) .... to retain their own (5) .... and traditions. They are very (6) .... hunters and fishermen and pass on the secrets of self-sufficiency from one (7) .... to another.

c Choose the best heading from the list (A–F) for each of the texts (1–3) in **b**.

A The ups and downs of driving abroad

B Keeping in touch with the past

C Tomorrow's world

D People and culture

E The legacy of mankind

F The joys of motoring

2 Read the text below. Use the word given in capitals at the end of each line to form a word that fits in the space in the same line. There is an example at the beginning **(0)**.

Despite the damage being done to the environment, the number of **(0)** ......*motorists*...... MOTOR
on the roads is constantly increasing. People think driving is far **(1)** .... PREFER
to taking public transport, or to cycling or walking, no matter the cost involved.
Apart from the expense of car **(2)** ...., there is also a price to be paid for MAINTAIN
the lack of physical exercise when relying on driving. It seems that national and
individual **(3)** .... is not always a good thing, as people are becoming PROSPER
more and more **(4)** .... dependent. In spite of this growing worry, TECHNOLOGY
many people will say that the car is **(5)** .... and it is an BENEFIT
(6) .... of success. INDICATE
People who are concerned about the environment and have an **(7)** .... of AWARE
the Earth's limited resources often put forward a **(8)** .... argument – CONTROVERSY
those who insist on driving their car into work or into the city centre should be
(9) .... by higher taxes or even fines. It seems that even drastic solutions PENALTY
like these won't persuade some drivers to give up the **(10)** .... and freedom DEPEND
they feel when using their car.

3 Read the text below and decide which answer **A**, **B**, **C** or **D** best fits each space.

Cairo, despite its contrasts, is similar to any other huge **(1)** .... jungle with its
high-rise tower blocks and evidence of urban development. It is a melting **(2)** ....
of people from all over Africa and, in parts, **(3)** .... a huge marketplace with little
(4) .... to move, as street vendors and customers haggle over the price of goods.
Cairo, however, is by no **(5)** .... a cheap city to visit, and accommodation, while
not costing the **(6)** ...., can be expensive. This is especially true if you want to stay
in one of the hotels along the **(7)** .... of the River Nile where there are long
(8) .... of unspoilt beauty. **(9)** .... in Cairo is relatively easy and cheap, as
admission to most sites is well within the average tourist's **(10)** .... All visitors to
Cairo **(11)** .... pleasure in experiencing the city and its sounds, and this is best
done on foot. Avoid cars, as this city of almost 16 million suffers from chronic traffic
(12) .... and the inevitable **(13)** .... which motor vehicles help to produce. For
a trip to the Pyramids, it is better to **(14)** .... a bus, provided you can **(15)** ....
the crowded and noisy conditions, as taxis can be expensive.

1	**A** concrete	**B** brick	**C** stone	**D** wooden
2	**A** box	**B** can	**C** pot	**D** pan
3	**A** looks	**B** resembles	**C** associates	**D** appears
4	**A** place	**B** area	**C** metres	**D** space
5	**A** ways	**B** means	**C** reasons	**D** costs
6	**A** earth	**B** world	**C** globe	**D** money
7	**A** sides	**B** grounds	**C** banks	**D** edges
8	**A** layers	**B** areas	**C** stretches	**D** line
9	**A** Viewing	**B** Sightseeing	**C** Journeying	**D** Sighting
10	**A** economics	**B** cost	**C** charge	**D** budget
11	**A** take	**B** enjoy	**C** get	**D** make
12	**A** queues	**B** lines	**C** congestion	**D** accidents
13	**A** dirt	**B** smog	**C** clouds	**D** exhaust
14	**A** book	**B** find	**C** rent	**D** catch
15	**A** give up	**B** put up with	**C** put up	**D** take in

Living conditions

Developing reading skills

Lead-in

1a Match the names of the different styles of housing (1–5) with the pictures (a–e).

1 a detached house   **4** a block of flats

2 terraced town houses   **5** a villa

3 a country cottage

b Work with a partner. Talk about the advantages and disadvantages of living in the houses in **a**. Use the following ideas to help you.

- a beautiful garden
- easy to look after
- expensive to maintain
- facilities within easy reach

- good to relax in
- hard to keep up
- in an attractive location
- noise problems

- old and charming
- quite cut off
- smart and modern

Which house would you prefer? Why?

2 Talk about where you live, using the language in the box to help you.

- in the centre of the city
- in a residential suburb
- on the outskirts of the city
- in a town or city with traditional architecture

- somewhere that has high-rise architecture
- in an area where there has been a lot of redevelopment
- in a rural village

3 Which of the factors in the lists below would be important for the following people (a–d)?

a somebody of your age

b a young, single, career-minded person

c someone with a family

d retired people

- parks and open spaces
- a good range of shops within walking distance
- within commuting distance to work
- a good community spirit
- lively nightlife

- a medical centre on the doorstep
- easy access to unspoilt countryside
- good public sports facilities nearby
- places of interest an easy drive or bus-ride away
- cultural facilities such as libraries, theatres and cinemas within easy reach
- within easy reach of schools
- little vandalism and violence
- peace and quiet

Make statements and give reasons for your answers.

e.g. *Having a medical centre on the doorstep would be important for retired people.*
As people get older, they feel they need to have medical facilities close by.

4 Match the beginnings of the newspaper headlines (1–5) with the correct endings (a–e).

1 Neighbours go to court over	**a** proposed housing development
2 New housing estate planned with	**b** historic building into flats
3 Village residents oppose	**c** new rent rises
4 Council wants to convert	**d** homes for fifty families
5 Tenants cannot afford	**e** dispute about noise

5 What do you think the houses of the future will be like? Think about the following aspects:

- the main living area
- the kitchen
- the sleeping area
- the power supply
- domestic entertainment facilities
- the heating

Strategy overview

Part 1: Multiple matching (headings)

When you do Part 1 of Paper 1, remember to apply the strategies and tips in this book.

DO	DON'T
✓ look for word groups to help you match the headings. (See Unit 1.)	✗ worry if you come across a word you do not know. You will probably still be able to find the right answer.
✓ look for word groups supported by examples to help you match the headings. (See Unit 5.)	✗ forget that one heading may be more suitable than another because it focuses on the gist of the paragraph and not on just one idea.
✓ focus on the gist (the main idea) of a paragraph to help you select the best heading for it. (See Unit 9.)	✗ match a heading to a paragraph because you see the same or similar words in both.
✓ look out for examples of figurative language in the headings. If you are unsure of the meaning, try to use the overall context to help you. (See Unit 13.)	

Exam time!

- You have 1 hour and 15 minutes for the whole of Paper 1, so you should allow just over 15 minutes to do each part of the exam.
- Before you attempt to match any of the headings, skim through the list of headings and the whole of the text.
- Return to the first paragraph you have to find a heading for. Read it again and then scan the list of headings to find the appropriate heading for the paragraph.
- As you match the headings to their paragraphs, write the headings on the reading text above the paragraphs you have matched them with.
- If you have difficulty finding a heading for a paragraph, move on. Return to this paragraph when you have found headings for the other paragraphs.
- Read the text through with the headings.
- Transfer your answers to the answer sheet before you move on to Part 2. You **will not** have time to do this at the end of the exam.

Exam practice: Part 1

You are going to read an article about homes in the next century. Choose the most suitable heading from the list **A–H** for each part **(1–6)** of the text. There is one extra heading which you do not need to use. There is an example at the beginning **(0)**.

A	Returning to the past
B	Houses will look very different
C	Saving valuable resources
D	Keeping an eye on how things are running
E	New directions in home design
F	Expensive and high-tech
G	Computers will control everything
H	Keeping you safe and sound

Houses of the twenty-first century

0   **E**

We are certain to see many exciting changes in home design in the new century. There are four main reasons why these changes will come about. We will be increasingly concerned about the environment; conventional energy sources will become expensive; we will probably become even more worried about security, and, above all, we will want to take advantage of 'smart' computer technology in home design. So far, this technology has only fed through into experimental houses and the expensive homes of the rich. In the new century, it will become available to the average homeowner.

1

The future will see the appearance of the intelligent house, incorporating a centralised computer management system. With smaller computers embedded in domestic appliances like microwave ovens, cookers, even future vacuum cleaners, the central computer will be able to send out instructions to start cooking the lunch or to clean up the house when it decides this needs to be done.

2

For an intelligent house to be able to look after itself, it will require a network of electronic sensors to send information back to the central computer, enabling the house to monitor the inside temperature and humidity and to ensure that the optimum levels of both are maintained. The house will also work out when it is time to water the garden, basing its decision on information flowing back to it from outside sensors about the levels of moisture in the flower beds and the lawn.

3

Future houses will not need to rely on their occupants to protect them against burglary by bolting doors and locking windows, because they will be able to protect themselves. Once the central computer learns that there is nobody at home, it will close any windows that may have been left open, lock all the doors and keep an eye out for burglars. If anyone tries to break in, it will alert the police or a security company. Needless to say, if the occupants have been careless enough to leave something burning on the cooker, the house will see to it that the fire is put out straightaway.

4

So far, we have made minimal use of solar energy in the average home, except for heating water in some of the sunnier countries. This is bound to change, however, as it becomes more anti-social to burn oil or even gas, and conventional fuels become more expensive as their supply starts to run out in the new century. In order to trap the maximum amount of available sunlight, it will be necessary to cover the exterior walls of houses with large areas of glazing. Consequently, the appearance of twenty-first century homes will be dominated by large expanses of glass.

5

Insulation will become a major concern in house design. New man-made materials will be used in house construction to cut down heat loss to the absolute minimum. The next generation of cooking appliances will require far less power than the appliances now to be found in homes. Computerised control will drastically reduce the amount of water used by the average household: dishwashers and washing machines will have to become much more efficient, as will showers and toilets. Gardens will be planned from the outset with water conservation in mind.

6

Architects' visions of twenty-first century urban landscapes with ultra high-rise towers connected by aerial travelways are slowly giving way to an alternative concept of communities of small, secure, self-contained living units. The majority of the public obviously dislike tower-block flats and would clearly prefer their own front door. It seems, therefore, that despite all the high-tech features of the homes of the next century, essentially, we may go back to the idea of the traditional house.

Language development

Word attack

1 Look back at the text on p.111. Focus on the three paragraphs after heading 4. Find the words and expressions that have the opposite meanings to the following words and expressions, as they are used in the text.

1 unusual ....

2 interior ....

3 natural ....

4 increase ....

5 wasteful ....

6 taking over from ....

7 integrated ....

8 modern ....

2 Look through the whole text on p.111 and find the words that mean the same as the following definitions.

1 relating to the home or family

2 electrical equipment used in people's homes

3 glass used for windows

4 using material to stop electricity, sound, heat, etc. from getting in or out

5 the process or method of building

6 all the people living together in the same house, flat, etc.

3 Complete the following text about approaches to house-building, using the words and expressions you found to complete **Exercises 1** and **2**.

In Britain, as in many other countries, the methods used to build small houses have hardly changed over hundreds of years. We still use (1) .... materials like stone and wood, and, unfortunately, the (2) .... in many new houses is so poor that huge amounts of heat are lost. True, most builders now fit double (3) .... in all the windows, but we need to do a lot more.

We should also start using more efficient methods of (4) .... For example, the (5) .... walls of houses could be manufactured in factories and assembled on the site. In this way, we could (6) .... the time it takes to build houses. I am sure that we will see bricks and wood slowly (7) .... special plastics and other (8) .... materials. Additionally, we need to recognise that the size of the modern (9) .... is getting smaller, with many families having only one child, so there is going to be an increased demand for small, (10) .... homes.

We have put a lot of thought into producing wonderful electrical (11) .... for our homes to make our lives easier. It's now time we put as much thought into how we build our homes.

Phrasal verbs

Complete the following statements, using the correct form of the phrasal verbs in the box.

| break in   come about   go back   see to   work out |

1 'This situation is a disgrace! The present housing crisis should never ....!'

2 'The government must .... a way to make houses affordable for everyone.'

3 'We must .... it that rent increases are brought under control.'

4 'We need secure homes that can't .... by burglars.'

5 'We must never .... to the terrible housing shortages this country has known in the past.'

Some uses of *keep*

1 Look at the example from the text on p.111.

... lock all the doors and **keep an eye out** *for burglars.*

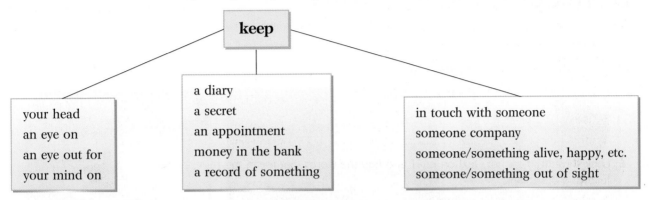

keep

your head
an eye on
an eye out for
your mind on

a diary
a secret
an appointment
money in the bank
a record of something

in touch with someone
someone company
someone/something alive, happy, etc.
someone/something out of sight

2 Rewrite the following sentences, replacing the words in *italics* with the correct form of *keep* and the expressions from the boxes.

1 He's got to learn to *concentrate* on his work.

....

2 After we met, we promised that we would *stay* in contact with each other.

....

3 The skill of the ambulance crew *stopped him dying* on the way to hospital.

....

4 We really must carefully *write down* our expenses, so that we know how much we are spending.

....

5 My friend was upset so I decided *to stay with her* during the evening.

....

6 Don't tell him anything personal because he *will go and tell it to everybody.*

....

Compound words with *house-* and *home-*

1 Combine the words in the box with *house-* and *home-* to form compound words. There is one word which can be combined with both *house-* and *home-*.

house-	home-
1	1
2	2
3	3
4	4
5	5

> **bound   grown   keeper   land   less   made
> proud   sick   warming   wife   work**

2 Complete the following sentences, using eight of the compound words from **Exercise 1**.

1 When I first moved away from the place where I grew up, I was often ....

2 Tom and Susan are so .... Whenever you drop in on them, everything in their flat looks absolutely perfect.

3 The return to more traditional foods had lead to an interest in .... bread and .... vegetables.

4 They've just moved into their new flat and they're having a .... party next week.

5 I was a .... and a mother for several years after my children were born, but staying at home every day, looking after the children and doing the .... really started to get me down.

6 There are always rows in our house because our children just refuse to do their .... and their teachers are always complaining.

7 It was terrible after I broke my leg because for two months I was totally .... I couldn't even get out to the local shops.

8 It's awful that there are literally millions of .... people in the world who have nowhere to live.

Science and technology

Developing reading skills

Lead-in

1a Match the names of the objects (1–6) with the photos (a–f).

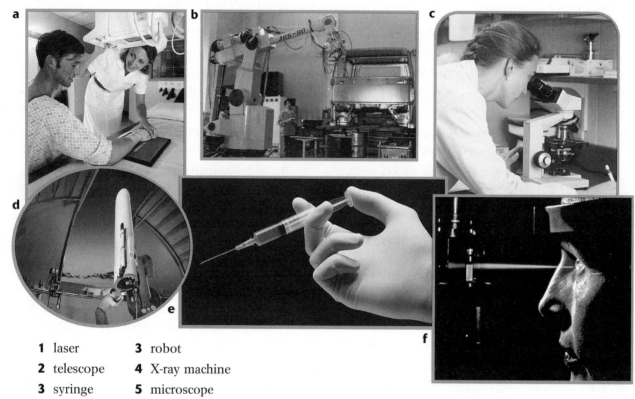

a b c d e f

1 laser   **3** robot

2 telescope   **4** X-ray machine

3 syringe   **5** microscope

b Which of the objects in **a** would you use if you wanted to:

- see if someone had broken a bone?
- make something tiny look larger?
- improve efficiency in a factory?
- take blood from someone or inject a medical drug into them?
- search for new planets and stars?
- perform a delicate medical operation or cut through a diamond?

2 How much do you know about famous scientists? Make statements about the people, choosing the correct information from the table.

Isaac Newton		radium
Charles Richter		the orbits of the planets
Marie Curie	devised	mathematical laws
Galileo	invented	the telescope
Jacques Cousteau	discovered	the aqualung (used in scuba diving)
Pythagoras		a sea route to India, going around Africa
Nicolaus Copernicus		the law of gravity
Vasco da Gama		a scale for measuring earthquakes

3 Match the verbs (1–8) with the nouns (a–h) to make statements about the work done by scientists.

1 perform

2 condition

3 apply

4 make

5 do

6 clone

7 automate

8 develop

a factories to make them work more efficiently with fewer people

b new drugs and vaccines to immunise people against diseases

c research into various scientific issues

d experiments to test their theories

e people and animals to behave in a certain way

f scientific knowledge to practical problems

g calculations based on statistical data

h plants and animals to make exact copies of them

4a Match the list of statements (1–6) with the scientific and technological developments (a–d) they refer to.

1 'This is a real breakthrough in medical science.'

2 'This will mean dangerous speeds of up to 25 km per hour.'

3 'This could cause the destruction of humanity.'

4 'This will make long distances seem like nothing.'

5 'This will give us immense power.'

6 'This will give people tremendous independence.'

a the splitting of the atom

b the discovery of penicillin

c the invention of the aeroplane

d the invention of the car

b Make statements about the advantages and disadvantages of automation and animal cloning, using the expression *on the one hand, … and on the other hand, …* Use the following ideas to help you.

- It has made factory production highly efficient.
- It could possibly be used on human embryos.
- It has given us the ability to standardise meat production.
- It has forced many people to work in dehumanising conditions.

Strategy overview

Part 2: Multiple choice

When you do Part 2 of Paper 1, remember to apply the strategies and tips in this book.

DO
✓ look for words and phrases of similar meanings in the text and in the answers to the questions. (See Unit 2.)
✓ look for implied meaning in the text when answering the questions. (See Unit 6.)
✓ look for reference sentences (sentences that refer back to important information contained earlier in the text) to help you answer the questions. (See Unit 10.)
✓ try to identify the writer's purpose in the text. (See Unit 14.)

DON'T
✗ forget that when a multiple-choice question is an incomplete sentence, the meaning of the whole sentence must match the text.
✗ leave a question unanswered. If you really cannot work out the answer to a question, guess!

Exam time!

- Allow about 15 minutes to do Part 2 of the exam.
- Skim through the text and questions before you attempt to answer any of the questions
- Read the text again and answer the questions. Spend a maximum of 8 minutes on this.
- If you cannot find the answers to any of the questions, move on.
- Check your answers. Look at the alternative answers and make sure they are wrong. Answer any questions you did not answer before.
- Transfer your answers to the answer sheet before you move on to Part 3 of the exam.

Exam practice: Part 2

You are going to read an extract from a famous novel about a future society. For Questions **1–7**, choose the answer (**A**, **B**, **C** or **D**) which you think fits best according to the text.

Inside a large, factory-like building, the Director of Hatcheries and Conditioning was addressing a group of young students as they followed him around the building.

He explained, 'Bokanovsky's process produces standard men and women and standardises the level of intelligence within each social group; the whole of a small factory can now be staffed with the products of a single human egg. Ninety-six identical Epsilon twins, for example, working ninety-six identical machines. Automation perfected.' He quoted the motto of the planet. 'Community, Identity, Stability.' Grand words.

'The aim is to create standard Gammas, unvarying Deltas, uniform Epsilons. Millions of identical twins. The principle of mass production at last applied to human biology.'

Of course, there was the problem of the modification of human embryos. Could a process be found to produce the same growth rate as in dogs and cows, but without defects? They had produced individuals who were full grown at six. A scientific triumph. But socially useless. Six-year-old men and women were too stupid to do even the simple, repetitive work of Epsilons. And the process was all or nothing; either you failed to modify at all, or else you modified the whole way. Scientists were still trying to find the ideal compromise between adults of twenty and adults of six. So far this had been a failure.

The visitors had arrived at Metre 170 on Rack 9. From this point onwards Rack 9 was enclosed and the bottles containing human embryos continued the remainder of their journey in a kind of tunnel, interrupted here and there by openings two or three metres wide.

'Heat conditioning,' explained Mr Foster, the young man who was in charge of this area.

Hot tunnels alternated with cold tunnels. Coolness was associated with discomfort in the form of hard X-rays. The embryos were learning the horror of cold. They would become adults who would go to the tropics, to become miners and steel workers. When they became small children, they would be taught to love heat, but now, as tiny embryos still in the bottles where they were developing, they were being taught to hate cold.

'And that,' stated the Director, 'is the secret of happiness and correct living – liking what you've *got* to do. All conditioning aims at that: making people like the work that society has chosen for them.'

In a gap between two tunnels, a nurse was delicately inserting a syringe into a passing bottle. The students stood watching her for a few moments in silence.

'Well, Lenina,' asked the young guide, 'What are you giving them?'

'Oh, the usual tropical diseases.'

'Tropical workers start being inoculated at Metre 150. We immunise them against future diseases,' explained Mr Foster.

On Rack 10, rows of the next generation of chemical workers were being trained in the toleration of lead, chlorine and other industrial chemicals, as they travelled along on a giant conveyor belt. The first batch of two hundred embryonic rocket-plane engineers were just passing the eleven hundredth meter mark on Rack 3. A special mechanism kept their containers in constant rotation. 'To improve their sense of balance,' Mr Foster explained. 'Doing repairs on the outside of rockets is a difficult job. We decrease the circulation of oxygen when they're the right way up, so they're half-starved of oxygen, and we double the flow when they're upside down. They learn to associate being the wrong way up with well-being; in fact, they're only truly happy when they're standing on their heads.'

'And now,' he continued, 'I'd like to show you some very interesting conditioning for Alpha-Plus intellectuals.'

1 The aim of Bokanovsky's process is to

   A increase the human population.

   B train men and women to do industrial work.

   C create skilled factory workers.

   D produce large numbers of people who are the same.

2 *Epsilons* must be

   A a type of human being produced for industrial work.

   B some kind of industrial machine.

   C people who are as stupid as simple animals.

   D adults with the minds of six-year-old children.

3 What had failed so far were attempts to produce

   A young and mature people.

   B humans that resembled animals.

   C twenty-year-olds with childish mentalities.

   D six-year-old children.

4 What happened at Metre 170 in the building?

   A People were being experimented on.

   B People were given injections against diseases.

   C Unborn human beings were prepared for their future lives.

   D Children were taught to like the jobs they would do in the future.

5 How were the future rocket-plane engineers being prepared for their jobs?

   A They were being exposed to special chemicals.

   B They were kept upside-down all the time.

   C They were being trained to live without oxygen.

   D They were being made to enjoy being upside-down.

6 The overall aim of what was going on inside the building seems to be

   A to use science to improve human health.

   B to use science to improve people's lives.

   C to use science to create human machines.

   D to help people cope with living in an industrial environment.

7 The writer's overall purpose is to

   A entertain his readers with an imaginative piece of science fiction.

   B warn readers about the dangers of scientific progress.

   C show that science cannot replace nature.

   D amuse readers by treating the issue of cloning humorously.

Language development

Word attack

Look back at the text on p.116. Focus on the sections of the text which begin *Inside a large …, The aim is to …, Of course, there was …,* and *On Rack 10, …* to find the words and expressions to complete the following text. Make any necessary changes. (The first letter of each missing word is given to help you.)

Many attempts have been made to use (1) m................................ p................................ methods in farming, most successfully in egg farming. Chickens spend their entire lives in tiny cages inside (2) f................-l................ buildings, where (3) c................................ b................................ carry their eggs the moment they are laid straight to the packing area in the building. Special (4) m................................ above every cage dispense food and water to the birds in carefully measured amounts.

Science has played its part by (5) m................................ chicken breeds to produce a bird that can lay eggs at the amazing (6) r................................ of up to 300 a year. Not only that, but the eggs each bird lays are of (7) u................................ size, and a (8) s................................ quality can be guaranteed in each (9) b................................ of eggs.

Many scientists and egg farmers claim that the birds are perfectly happy living in this way. Opponents say that the animals' (10) w................-b................ must be affected by such unnatural conditions.

Preposition + noun + preposition

1 Look at the example from the text on p.116.

*… the young man who was **in charge of** this area.*

2 Complete the following sentences, using the phrases in the box.

> **in case of   in charge of   in control of   in danger of   in fear of   in place of in sight of   in terms of   on account of   on behalf of**

1 The famous scientist accepted the award .... of his entire research team.

2 A researcher has announced that she believes her team are .... a major development in treating cancer.

3 Many workers feel they are .... being replaced by industrial robots.

4 Professor James is .... the Linguistics Department.

5 I had to stand up and give a short speech .... the guest lecturer who had to cancel at the last minute.

6 Technologists at the power station where the accident occurred say they are now completely .... the situation.

7 This has been a highly successful project, both .... the results we have achieved and the team spirit we have had all along.

8 A team of scientists in the Himalayas have had to abandon their experiments .... the terrible weather conditions they have met with.

9 When the rocket exploded, spectators ran as fast as they could .... their lives.

10 All laboratories have instructions about what to do .... fire.

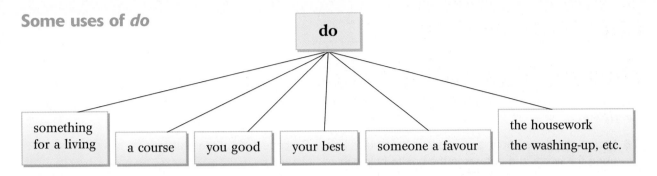

Some uses of *do*

do

something for a living • a course • you good • your best • someone a favour • the housework the washing-up, etc.

Complete the following sentences with the correct form of *do* and the expressions from the boxes. Make any necessary changes.

1 I'd been working half the night in the laboratory and I thought a short walk would

....

2 Our daughter .... in computing at the moment.

3 Don't worry if you can't find the answers to all the questions. Just ....

4 Could you ...., please, and help me with this experiment?

5 What does he ....? Oh, he's a mechanical engineer.

6 We are both computer programmers and we're out at work all day, so when we get home in the evening we have a lot of household chores in front of us, like

....

Use of English

Read the following text and decide which answer **A**, **B**, **C** or **D** best fits each space.

Science promises to change our lives in many ways in the twenty-first century. Most people probably **(1)** .... future scientific **(2)** .... with travelling to distant planets or with the host of new **(3)** .... that will be available in twenty-first-century homes. However, it is probably in the **(4)** .... of medicine that science will have the greatest **(5)** .... on people's lives. **(6)** .... is going on to find ways to **(7)** .... people against AIDS, which has claimed the lives of so many young people, and to **(8)** .... cures for terrible **(9)** .... like cancer. Of course, before any of these are made available to the public, they will have been thoroughly **(10)** ....

1	**A** connect	**B** link	**C** associate	**D** join
2	**A** developments	**B** progresses	**C** improvement	**D** advance
3	**A** mechanisms	**B** gadgets	**C** instruments	**D** machines
4	**A** subject	**B** department	**C** region	**D** field
5	**A** impact	**B** force	**C** change	**D** affect
6	**A** Research	**B** Investigation	**C** Studying	**D** Analysis
7	**A** inject	**B** immunise	**C** defend	**D** cure
8	**A** invent	**B** locate	**C** discover	**D** make
9	**A** diseases	**B** illnesses	**C** sicknesses	**D** infections
10	**A** proven	**B** tried	**C** checked	**D** tested

Education and learning

Developing reading skills

Lead-in

1a Look at the three learning situations in the photos below. Describe each of the situations, using the words and phrases in the box to help you.

a

b

> **a learning tool   access on-line information**
> **a mixed school   a single sex school**
> **independent learning   interactive learning**
> **teacher-centred   traditional**
> **dull   motivating**

c

b Which learning situation would you prefer to be in? Why?

2 Match the statements (1–6) with the photos in **1a**.

1 'I can learn just about everything I want right here, so I don't need teachers.'

2 'We used to dread coming to class but now learning is much more exciting.'

3 'I believe that mixed classes are undoubtedly preferable for successful learning.'

4 'A situation like this requires funding from the government to buy the technology.'

5 'A strict classroom environment is necessary to ensure successful learning.'

6 'Computers are the tutors of the future and can provide students with all the information they need.'

3 Do you agree/disagree with the following aspects of using a computer in learning situations? Give reasons for your answers.

- It provides creative and liberating learning possibilities.
- It can make mock tests more efficient.
- It is an efficient tool for self-directed learning.
- Assignments can be done through access to the Internet.
- The role of the teaching staff is the same.
- It provides for a knowledge-based curriculum.
- The student can work at his or her own pace.
- It isn't necessary to learn things by heart.

4 Answer the following questions.

1 What are the entrance requirements to get into university in your country?

2 Until what age is attendance at secondary school compulsory in your country?

3 Do many young people attend extra lessons outside normal school in your country? Why?/Why not?

Strategy overview

Part 3: Gapped text

When you do Part 3 of Paper 1, remember to apply the strategies and tips in this book.

DO	DON'T
✓ look for reference words like *it, him, her, they, this*, etc., which can refer to words before or after the gaps in the text. Use these words to help you match the missing parts to the main text. (See Unit 3.)	✗ choose your answers too quickly.
✓ look for words and ideas in the missing sentences which are associated to the main text to help you match the missing parts. (See Unit 7.)	✗ worry about not understanding specific words in the text. Use the context to help you understand words you don't recognise.
✓ look for words and phrases which connect ideas to help you understand how the text fits together, e.g. *As a result* introduces an effect of an action or situation. (See Unit 11.)	✗ choose an answer just because a particular word is used in both the main text and the missing text.
✓ look for words and phrases which give additional information, e.g. *also, additionally, besides*, etc. to help you understand how the text fits together. (See Unit 15.)	

Exam time!

- Allow about 15 minutes to do Part 3 of the exam.
- Look at the whole task first before you start to choose your answers.
- Do what you think are the easy questions first and deal with the problem areas last.
- If you get stuck, move on to the next question.
- Be prepared to spend longer on the middle questions in the gapped text, as these are often the ones which are more difficult.
- Transfer your answers to the answer sheet as you proceed through the questions.
- Never leave a question unanswered. If you cannot find the answer to a question, guess!

Exam practice: Part 3

You are going to read an article about a scheme to help educate students who do not attend regular lessons at school. Eight sentences have been removed from the article. Choose from the sentences **A–I** the one which fits each gap **(1–7)**. There is one extra sentence which you do not need to use. There is an example at the beginning **(0)**.

Technology and learning

Each term, an increasing number of young people are excluded from school in Britain for a range of reasons including truancy, expulsion, or because their parents' work involves travelling. Some academics now believe that the 'virtual classroom', using computer networks, could be the best way to lure these young people back to some form of learning. **0** **G**

Currently, in most local authorities, the availability of 'home tuition' ranges from sparse to non-existent. The results of this are predictable. **1** By the time he is 20, he will be living on state benefits or on the proceeds of pickpocketing or burglaries.

The tragedy is that John knows all this very well. He is perfectly aware that the successful pupils he makes fun of and bullies are likely to be the winners in the end. The bus in the distance, though visible and brightly lit, has left him behind. **2**

Suppose, though, that someone brought him a computer with software that set him interesting work to do at home, at his own pace, without fear of failure or ridicule, where he could pick and choose from different subjects. He could contact a tutor when he needed help and chat to other pupils in his group from the peace and quiet of his home. **3** Treated seriously by adults, he might regain some pride and belief in himself. He might eventually sit a few exams and get some qualifications and actually do quite well.

4 The point is that nobody will know until someone gives the idea a proper trial, with good equipment and software, high-quality teachers and adequate funding. This autumn, a team led by Stephen Heppell of Anglia University's Ultralab is going to do just that.

The plan is to start with a pilot group of 30 teenagers who are not in full-time education for a variety of reasons. **5** Much has to be worked out, which is why this is a pilot project. 'We need to put together a toolkit for what works – methodology and pedagogy,' says Heppell.

6 Exactly what will on-screen tasks look like? What about pupils with literacy problems? Who will be the tutors? How will targets be set, and what about the pupils who drop out – as some, presumably, will? 'There will be failure for some,' says Heppell, 'and we have to think how to manage that.'

In a sense, all of these problems, though they demand attention, add up to theoretical detail. The real issues, however, concern a change in the willingness and positive attitudes in the government and educational bodies. If this is to be achieved, then all those involved will be acknowledging that school is not the only answer and that there are other routes to learning. **7**

The Ultralab scheme has influential support from those who see it as a means of attacking truancy and exclusion. Arguably, though, it will also question some of the assumptions about formal schooling.

A They will be given state-of-the-art hardware, video and audio facilities, and they will be grouped into fours, each group sharing a tutor.

B Similarly, it will become apparent that if a participative approach to learning works better for marginalised pupils, then it will work for others too.

C So, he makes his mark in the only way he can and, in doing so, he feels worthless and miserable.

D Take John, for example; he is permanently excluded, too far behind to be successful in another school and drifting into criminal circles.

E Or, of course, it might all end in tears and failure yet again.

F Theoretically, this sounds fine but the number of still unanswered questions is almost bewildering.

G Such a scheme would provide the pupils with access to education while they are at home.

H This is an example of how not to use a potentially powerful resource.

I Were this to happen, he might stay in and work and begin to feel part of a learning community.

Language development

Word attack

Complete the following sentences, using the words in the box. Make any necessary changes.

> **bully funding literacy pace qualifications state-of-the-art truancy tutor**

1 The government has launched a .... program to help children who have problems with reading and writing.

2 Parents are being encouraged to make sure their children attend school in an attempt to bring down .... levels.

3 I need extra help in some subjects, so I have a private .... who comes to my house.

4 My son refused to go to school because he .... by an older boy.

5 People who fail at school can still get .... late in life at colleges or through home-learning schemes.

6 One of the biggest problems in giving children access to computers in school is the lack of ....

7 There is no point in having .... technology if children are not motivated to learn.

8 I much prefer working on my own than in a big group, because I can make progress at my own ....

Word pairs

1 Look at the example from the text on p.122.

... *where he could* **pick and choose** *from different subjects.*

2 Complete the following sentences, using the words in the box to form common word pairs.

> **again figures miss parcel quiet tired**

1 According to the facts and .... given by the Ministry of Education, more and more girls are taking science subjects.

2 A good education is part and .... of the development of each individual.

3 After having failed the exams twice, he was sick and .... of studying.

4 Choosing the best subjects for a good career can be a case of hit and ....

5 Maria needs to have peace and .... when she is studying.

6 Now and .... he regrets not having worked harder at school.

Expressions with *make*

1 Look at the example from the text on p.122.

the successful pupils he **makes fun of** *and bullies*

2 Rewrite the following sentences using the correct form of *make* and the word in **bold**.

1 I'm sorry, I didn't mean to take your book.
mistake
I'm sorry I .... by taking your book.

2 'I will try harder next term,' said the girl.
promise
The girl .... try harder next term.

3 All the students have done well this term.
progress
All the students .... this term.

4 The teacher told the class to be very quiet.
noise
The teacher told the class ....

5 You must try to do all the questions in the examination.
attempt
You must .... all the questions in the examination.

Error correction

Read the text below and look carefully at the <u>underlined</u> words which are not correct. Write the correct words

One of the most difficult times at school is when we have to <u>make</u> exams. It's even worse when they are important and we need to <u>take</u> them with good <u>notes</u>, especially if we want to get into university or go on to further <u>reading</u>. Most students feel anxious and tense before an exam and this can sometimes lead to students not reading the <u>directions</u> for the paper they are taking. Additionally, they do not <u>give</u> attention to the time allowed for each paper. Many exam <u>applicants</u> fail because they have not left themselves sufficient time to <u>view</u> their work. Most students <u>do</u> some errors in the exam and need time at the end to go over what they have written. This is true in whatever school <u>field</u> you are doing an exam in.

Use of English

1 Read the following text and decide which answer **A**, **B**, **C** or **D** best fits each space.

Most children in Britain start **(1)** .... school at the age of five and spend the next eleven years in **(2)** .... In some parts of the country, pupils have to **(3)** .... an examination or test at the age of eleven to see what kind of **(4)** .... school they should go to. However, in most parts of the country, this examination does not exist and all the local students go to a **(5)** .... school, regardless of class, colour or sex.

When students finish school, they can go on to a college or university. There has been a growth in **(6)** .... at such institutions since the 1980s and Britain is now producing more **(7)** .... from its universities and colleges than in the past. Universities and colleges produce their own **(8)** .... describing the courses they offer, which gives British students information about places of study outside their home town.

Courses for adults are usually **(9)** .... in the evenings as most adults work during the day. They offer a very wide range of subjects and **(10)** .... for such courses are usually relatively low.

1	**A** kindergarten	**B** high	**C** primary	**D** private
2	**A** learning	**B** studies	**C** classrooms	**D** education
3	**A** make	**B** sit	**C** pass	**D** read
4	**A** junior	**B** higher	**C** comprehensive	**D** secondary
5	**A** senior	**B** comprehensive	**C** new	**D** public
6	**A** enlisting	**B** enrolment	**C** joining	**D** writing
7	**A** graduates	**B** degrees	**C** professors	**D** tutors
8	**A** brochures	**B** essays	**C** timetables	**D** prospectuses
9	**A** run	**B** set	**C** made	**D** placed
10	**A** prices	**B** charges	**C** fees	**D** bills

2 Read the text below. Use the word given in capitals at the end of each line to form a word that fits in the space in the same line. There is an example at the beginning (**0**).

Nowadays, the standard requirement for university **(0)** ...*entrance*... is	ENTER
three 'A-level' passes, although some universities will accept less.	
It has been seen that some students who are **(1)** .... at school	EXCEL
throughout the years are faced with **(2)** .... when they sit these exams.	FAIL
For such students, **(3)** .... at a local technical college enables them to	ENROL
carry on in education and for some who transfer to university later, **(4)**	GRADUATE
becomes a reality. Getting academic **(5)** .... is becoming increasingly	QUALIFY
important in the competitive world of work and that is why **(6)** .... at	ATTEND
places of higher and further education is rising.	

Museums

Developing reading skills

Lead-in

1 Look at the two photos of museums. Describe the differences between them, using the words in the box.

> atmosphere   discover   educational   exhibit   exhibition   formal
> fun   interactive   motivating   quiet   traditional

2 Read quickly through the following short descriptions of three museums. Do not worry about the words you do not recognise. Match the names of the museums to the correct text. There is one extra name you do not need to use.

1 Aviation Museum   **3** Historic Dockyard

2 Heritage Museum   **4** Battle Museum

a
> The legacy of shipbuilding skills can still be felt and seen throughout this award-winning museum. Its five galleries and other attractions all add to your experience and enjoyment of this unique site. There is a fine collection of sails and flags, together with memorabilia on the launch of the HMS Victory and its maiden voyage.

b
> The Museum, open since 1982, tells the story of flying from the earliest days to the present time. Exhibits include models of planes from the past, the bouncing bomb, uniform and armaments displays. Permanently housed in the museum are two fighter planes which participated in the Battle of Britain.

c
> Dazzling treasures of outstanding beauty and elegant craftsmanship from one of the world's most famous museums are on display. Focusing on one of the most brilliant periods in the evolution of English art and craftsmanship, the exhibition includes a priceless collection of English silver as well as other magnificent objects. There are several hands-on features including coin minting, brass rubbing and a flintlock musket.

3 Work with a partner and answer the following questions.

   1 What can you see in the most famous museums in your country?

   2 Do you think museums in your country could be improved? How?

   3 Why is it important to have museums?

Strategy overview

Part 4: Multiple matching (questions)

When you do Part 4 of Paper 1, remember to apply the strategies and tips in this book.

DO	DON'T
✓ look for additional information which is given through relative clauses to help you match the questions to the correct text. (See Unit 4.)	✗ forget that when you find information that relates to a question, there may be similar information in other sections of the text which you might need to use to help you decide on the correct answer.
✓ look for words and phrases which have a similar meaning to those in the questions. (See Unit 8.)	✗ forget there are similarities between sections of the text and that you need to make sure you have identified the right section for each particular question.
✓ look for words and phrases which introduce examples of items referred to in the questions. (See Unit 12.)	
✓ look for words in the text that show an opinion or attitude. (See Unit 16.)	

Exam time!

- Allow about 15 minutes to do Part 4 of the exam.
- Read the title of the text to get an idea of the main topic you are going to read about.
- Read the questions very carefully first. Then select the part(s) of the text where you need to scan for specific details.
- Remember that some answers can be found in more than one section.
- You do not need to answer the questions in sequence. If you find one difficult, leave it and move on to the next.
- Don't choose an answer just because it has the same words as the question.
- Transfer your answers to the answer sheet as you go along, so that you don't run out of time at the end of the exam.

Exam practice: Part 4

You are going to read extracts from descriptions of six different museums. For Questions **1–14**, choose from museums **(A–F)**. The museums may be chosen more than once. When more than one answer is required, these may be given in any order. There is an example at the beginning **(0)**.

Which museum

contains present-day exhibits?

provides activities to develop character?

could show you what life was like in Europe in the past?

encourages visitors to use computers to find information?

might an archaeologist enjoy most?

would enable a visitor to learn about different tribes of people?

suggests that the activities provided may influence someone's choice of career?

was created to promote achievement in a certain field?

has recently been redecorated?

has exhibits of hunted wildlife?

has staff who dress up to look like celebrities?

links what is on display to what children study in school?

offers an exhibition based on a mythical character?

| 0 | **F** |

| 1 | |

| 2 | | 3 | |

| 4 | | 5 | |

| 6 | |

| 7 | |

| 8 | |

| 9 | |

| 10 | |

| 11 | |

| 12 | |

| 13 | |

| 14 | |

Museums

A The Children's Museum

One of America's largest, most unique children's museums is visited by 100,000 members of the public each year. Set in an imaginary town, young people begin to better understand the world through exploration and role-play. Some even sow the seeds of future ambitions as they act out dozens of different occupations. The museum offers exciting hands-on activities which help to build self-esteem and confidence, as well as allowing adults to become part of the educational process. The museum has become a favourite field trip for schools, youth groups and scouts.

B The Victoria and Albert Museum

Unrivalled as the world's finest museum of decorative arts, London's Victoria and Albert Museum was founded in 1852 to support and encourage excellence in art and design. It is home to 145 galleries, including the national collections of sculpture, furniture, fashion and textiles, paintings, silver, glass, ceramics, jewellery, books, prints and photographs. The magnificent collections constitute a unique international resource. Some four million objects are held by the museum, ranging from the English landscape artist, Constable, to oriental ceramics, and the finest collection of Italian Renaissance sculpture outside Italy, as well as the most impressive collection of Indian art and artefacts outside the subcontinent.

C The Natural History Museum

Why not discover more about the natural world through music, art and drama in a range of special events and hands-on workshops? At the Earth Galleries, you can see the Museum's permanent exhibitions relating to the planet. At one of these galleries, the Earth Lab, investigate the impressive diversity of British geology, and compare your own fossils, rocks and minerals with the Museum's reference collection, object displays and multimedia database. One of the Museum's most popular galleries has now reopened after undergoing a major face-lift. It includes old favourites such as the giant robotic scorpion and live leafcutter ant colony, as well as exciting new elements from the Museum's collection of over 30 million species of insects and other arthropods.

D The Museum of the Moving Image

The magical world of film and television comes to life before your eyes at the Museum of the Moving Image. Here, *you* are the star! You can fly like Superman, become a newsreader, audition for a Hollywood screen role, watch hundreds of films and TV clips, and interact with our cast of actor guides. Crossing the drawbridge entrance of our new special exhibition, you can step back through the mists of time to enter the magical world of King Arthur and his Knights of the Round Table. There are hands-on exhibits and a multimedia touchscreen which amazingly allows you to interact with the world around you.

E Quex House Museum

Quex is one of Kent's finest Regency houses and museums. A vast collection of treasures from different civilisations including splendid pieces of oriental furniture, rugs, ornaments and clocks gathered on expeditions to Africa has been assembled at Quex, making this an exciting place to visit and an important centre for the academic study of different races. In the eight galleries at Quex, you will find an amazing variety of items from the finest animal specimens in the world to striking tribal art, weapons, carvings and costumes, as well as valuable collections of Chinese porcelain and local architecture.

F Maidstone Museum and Art Gallery

Let us introduce you to a wealth of heritage. This exceptionally fine regional museum, housed in a delightful Elizabethan manor house, boasts a rich and impressive variety of historical objects, fine art and natural history. Fine and decorative arts include European and British paintings, ceramics, glass, furniture, costume and textiles from the 17th to 20th centuries. An extensive collection contrasts artefacts from the Prehistoric Roman, Anglo-Saxon and Medieval periods, and an Egyptian collection including our own mummy. The curator of the museum provides a stimulating range of contemporary and historical exhibitions with an educational programme linked to history and science.

Language development

Word attack

1 Look back at the texts on p.129. Find the words that mean the same as the following definitions.

Text A

1 interactive ....

2 role-play (verb) ....

Text B

3 none other like it ....

4 types of cloth ....

Text C

5 variety ....

6 not temporary ....

Text D

7 to give a short performance in order to try and get a part in a play, etc.

....

8 the people who act in a film or play ....

Text E

9 huge ....

10 brought together ....

Text F

11 located ....

12 modern ....

2 Complete the following sentences, using eight of the words from **Exercise 1**.
Make any necessary changes.

1 I went for an .... but was disappointed to hear I hadn't got the part.

2 We adore looking at silks from different parts of the world, so we always head for the .... gallery in any museum.

3 The children's visit to the national history exhibition was great fun – they spent some time .... historical characters like kings, queens and traitors.

4 Allow enough time to look at all the exhibits – we have more than 500 items to look at .... in five galleries.

5 A lot of children find history books a bit dull, but if you take them to a good museum, they often find the whole subject a lot more ....

6 Museums are a good way of seeing artefacts .... from the four corners of the world all under one roof.

7 I really enjoy the .... approach of modern museums – you learn so much more by touching, hearing and really experiencing the exhibits.

8 The museum said it had an .... collection of modern art, but we found the exhibition rather disappointing.

Use of English

1 Read the text below. Use the word given in capitals at the end of each line to form a word that fits in the space in the same line. There is an example at the beginning **(0)**.

In Britain, many larger museums offer **(0)** _educational_ activities for	EDUCATION
school students. These include the **(1)** .... of	PRESENT
aspects of permanent collections in a way which is **(2)**	ACCESS
to younger learners. Special **(3)** .... emphasise the social	EXHIBIT
and **(4)** .... aspects of the lives of people in different	CULTURE
settings across the ages. There is often a focus on human	
(5) .... and development.	CREATE
Museums like the Victoria and Albert run a major programme	
in the study of **(6)** .... arts, while others focus on	DECORATE
learning through **(7)** .... with the object in question.	ACT
Such a hands-on approach adds to the **(8)** .... of seeing	EXCITE
the object close up and **(9)** .... the visitor to participate	ABLE
in a meaningful learning experience. Many hands-on activities revolve around	
an **(10)** .... world where the participant takes on different roles.	IMAGINE

2 Read the text below and decide which answer **A**, **B**, **C** or **D** best fits each space.

Available to all museum **(1)** .... is a vast array of artefacts and **(2)** .... which have been **(3)** .... from all over the world. The **(4)** .... of most museums are usually very proud of the **(5)** .... in their museums and are always willing to provide information about them. Museums enable the **(6)** .... to enjoy the artefacts they house through **(7)** .... which are often changed on a regular basis, or are in the permanent **(8)** ...., where large collections of different objects and sometimes paintings are on **(9)** .... Many European museums are home to **(10)** .... works of art such as the *Mona Lisa* in the Louvre museum in Paris.

1	**A** flocks	**B** audiences	**C** spectators	**D** visitors
2	**A** treasures	**B** porcelain	**C** displays	**D** arts
3	**A** collected	**B** awarded	**C** borrowed	**D** removed
4	**A** curators	**B** inspectors	**C** leaders	**D** masters
5	**A** items	**B** ceramics	**C** expeditions	**D** guides
6	**A** public	**B** individuals	**C** population	**D** groups
7	**A** lectures	**B** presentations	**C** auditions	**D** exhibitions
8	**A** floors	**B** homes	**C** galleries	**D** libraries
9	**A** display	**B** loan	**C** sight	**D** exhibits
10	**A** worthless	**B** expensive	**C** priceless	**D** rich

1a Complete the table with the correct words from the box. Some words can fit in more than one category.

apply attendance breakthrough clone community curriculum discover essay experiment fail field high-rise literacy nightlife qualification rent research residential subject suburb vandalism

Science and technology	Living conditions	Education

b Complete the following short texts with the words from **a**. Make any necessary changes.

1 A few years ago, a team of scientists (1) .... a way to successfully (2) .... a sheep, producing a lamb which had the same genetic make-up as its 'mother'. This (3) .... in biological science could (4) .... to farming methods in the 21st century. It has the potential to standardise meat production by standardising the animals themselves. There are, however, many people who feel uneasy about (5) .... on animals in this way, feeling that it is interfering with nature. Some even think that all (6) .... into cloning should be stopped, as it may end in scientists cloning a human. It is undoubtedly a controversial (7) .... of science which requires careful debate.

2 In city centres, people often have to pay high (1) .... to live in a small flat in a (2) .... block. This style of housing is also often linked to social problems like (3) ...., with local youths damaging cars and other property. On the other hand, the most exciting (4) .... is often to be found in the centres of cities, making them attractive to people of all ages. There are also benefits to living outside the city centre in quiet (5) .... and (6) .... areas. These include a greater sense of (7) .... spirit and more access to parks and places to walk.

3 Even in countries where school (1) .... is compulsory up to the age of sixteen or more, low levels of (2) .... persist, with many children not learning to read and write fluently. These children often (3) .... exams which require them to write long (4) .... to answer the exam questions. This is not necessarily an indication of intelligence or talent, as many such children do well in mathematics and more practical (5) .... like Information Technology. This has been added to the (6) .... in many schools, providing children with an important (7) .... for when they join the computerised world of work.

c Choose the best heading from the list (A–F) for each of the texts (1–3) in **b**.

A Scientists help animals **D** A threat to humanity or an answer to food problems?
B Getting out of the city **E** Persistent problems and new developments
C Where to live in the city **F** Schools fail pupils

2 Read the text below. Use the word given in capitals at the end of each line to form a word that fits in the space in the same line. There is an example at the beginning **(0)**.

Museums, with their diverse **(0)** ....*collections*...., can offer visitors a wealth of	COLLECT
(1) .... in fields ranging from state-of-the-art space exploration to	KNOW
(2) .... history. It is essential, therefore, that schools do not overlook the	NATURE
huge educational value of these institutions. For one thing, many museums are able	
to offer their young visitors an **(3)** .... into something they should all find	SIGHT
interesting – the **(4)** .... of their own culture and society.	EVOLVE
It is true that many museums can be criticised for their **(5)** .... in the past	FAIL
to attract young visitors but **(6)** .... steps are being taken to remedy this	IMPRESS
by providing hands-on, interactive exhibits which draw huge crowds.	
No longer are museum visitors just passive **(7)** .... of the displays in the	OBSERVE
museum. Instead, they become **(8)** .... in a variety of activities laid on	PARTICIPATE
for them by the museum staff. Museums have also been working hard on	
(9) .... to their general facilities, such as information and library services,	IMPROVE
quiet study areas, and refreshments. With **(10)** .... developments showing	TECHNOLOGY
no signs of slowing, who knows what the museum of the future will have to offer?	

3 Read the text below and decide which answer **A**, **B**, **C** or **D** best fits each space.

Since the arrival of modern construction **(1)** ...., architects have come in for a certain amount of criticism from the general **(2)** .... They are often accused of only applying what they learn on their university **(3)** .... courses which is to design massive tower blocks that people don't want to live in. The **(4)** .... in some of these buildings say they get **(5)** .... and tired of trying to use lifts that break down all the time and, up on the twentieth floor, they feel cut **(6)** .... from the local community. In some cases, they have complained that the **(7)** .... in the buildings is so poor that they have to live in damp conditions for much of the year.

Architects, for their part, say they do their **(8)** .... to provide **(9)** .... for people at reasonable costs and this is very difficult in **(10)** .... areas where the cost of land is **(11)** .... high.

There are changes taking place, however. In **(12)** .... of large blocks of flats, smaller low-rise buildings are being designed with a reasonable amount of **(13)** .... space around them and facilities **(14)** .... easy reach. This approach has already proven to be very popular. The new **(15)** .... owners or tenants say they feel they have a real sense of privacy and independence.

1	**A** ways	**B** means	**C** methods	**D** procedures
2	**A** people	**B** public	**C** citizens	**D** community
3	**A** diploma	**B** certificate	**C** qualification	**D** degree
4	**A** locals	**B** inhabitants	**C** householders	**D** residents
5	**A** sick	**B** miserable	**C** weary	**D** upset
6	**A** out	**B** off	**C** up	**D** away
7	**A** insulation	**B** protection	**C** isolation	**D** separation
8	**A** most	**B** greatest	**C** best	**D** largest
9	**A** houses	**B** residences	**C** places	**D** homes
10	**A** civil	**B** urban	**C** political	**D** metropolitan
11	**A** exceptionally	**B** definitely	**C** outstandingly	**D** impressively
12	**A** part	**B** stead	**C** place	**D** position
13	**A** open	**B** free	**C** clear	**D** wide
14	**A** inside	**B** within	**C** at	**D** with
15	**A** housebound	**B** household	**C** housekeeping	**D** houseproud

Mini-dictionary

Unit 1

adventure a journey, experience, etc., that is strange and exciting and often dangerous

crew all the people working on a ship, plane, spacecraft, etc.

dawn the time at the beginning of the day when light first appears

fulfil an ambition to do what you have planned to do in life

glide to move smoothly and quietly, as if no effort was being made

hang glider a large frame covered with cloth that you hold on to and fly slowly through the air on, without an engine

land to arrive on the ground from the air

parachute a circular piece of cloth fastened by thin ropes to people or objects that are dropped from aircraft in order to make them fall slowly

risk your life to put your life in danger

sleeping bag a large warm bag for sleeping in when camping

sunset the time of the day when the sun disappears and night begins

tent a movable shelter made of cloth or plastic material supported by a structure of poles and ropes used by campers

unique being the only one of its kind

view what you can see from a particular place

waterproof not allowing water to go through

Unit 2

be keen on to like very much

beat to defeat someone completely, e.g. in a game or competition

champion someone or something that has won a competition, especially in sport

court an area specially made for playing ball games, e.g. tennis

get on someone's nerves to annoy or upset someone

get rid of to make someone leave because you do not like them or because they are causing problems

have a word with someone to talk with someone, usually to give advice or a warning about something

lose not to win a game or match

make your mind up to decide to do something

miss to fail to hit, catch, find, meet, touch, hear, see, etc.

not be able to stand something to be unable to accept, usually someone's behaviour or a difficult or annoying situation

pitch a specially marked out area of ground on which a sport is played, e.g. football

put you off something to discourage someone from doing something

score to gain one or more points in a sport, game, competition, etc.

skill an ability to do something well, especially because you have learned or practised it

win to be the best or first in a competition, race, game, etc.

Unit 3

at your fingertips easily available

capacity the amount that something can hold or contain

e-mail a system that allows people to send messages to each other by computer

field a subject or topic of study

hardware the machinery which makes up a computer, as opposed to the systems that make it perform particular jobs

keyboard a row or several rows of keys on a musical instrument or a machine

monitor the screen which is used with a computer

multimedia using a mixture of sound, pictures, film and writing to give information, especially with computers

on-line connected to the Internet through a telephone and modem

run to operate a computer program

site a document or set of documents, often with pictures, that you can look at on a computer which is connected to the Internet

software the set of systems (in the form of programs rather than machine parts) which controls the operation of a computer

the turn of the century at the end of the old century and the beginning of the new one

virus a set of instructions secretly put into a computer, that can destroy information stored in the computer

Unit 4

allergy a medical condition in which you become ill or you get a rash because you have eaten certain foods, touched certain things, etc.

anxious very worried about something

bandage a long narrow piece of material for tying round a part of the body that has been hurt

be prone to to be likely to do something or suffer from something

calm down to become quiet after strong emotion or nervous activity

cope with to deal successfully with a difficult situation

cure a medicine or medical treatment that can make an illness disappear

infection a disease caused by bacteria or a virus that affects a particular part of your body

injection an act of giving a drug by using a special needle

injury physical hurt or damage caused to your body, especially by an accident or attack

prescription a piece of paper on which a doctor writes what medicine a person should have

rash a lot of red spots on someone's skin caused by an illness

sedentary involving a lot of sitting down

symptom a physical condition that shows you have an illness

wound an injury, especially a cut or a hole made in your skin by a knife, bullet, etc.

Unit 5

bargain something bought cheaply or for less than its usual price

browse to look through or read parts of a book, magazine, etc. without a particular purpose

cash money in the form of notes and coins rather than cheques, credit cards, etc.

consumer a person who buys and uses goods and services

department store a large shop divided into departments, each selling different types of things

deposit a sum of money which is the first payment for something so that it will be kept for you

discount a reduction in the cost of something you are buying

goods articles for sale

refund a sum of money that is given back to you

satisfied pleased because something has happened in the way you want

save up for to keep and add to an amount of money for later use

shop around for to compare the price and quality of different things before you decide which to buy

try on to put on a piece of clothing to see if it fits you or if it suits you

window-shopping the activity of looking at goods in shop windows without necessarily intending to buy

Unit 6

account an arrangement that you have with a bank to pay in and take out money

afford to be able to buy or pay for

borrow to use something that belongs to someone else and that you must give back to them later

broke having no money

cash a cheque to exchange a cheque for the amount of money written on it

change your mind to change your opinion or decision about something

earn to receive a particular amount of money for the work you do

have your eye on to have noticed something that you want to buy or have

hold your breath to stop breathing for a short while

hold your tongue to be quiet and not say anything to anyone

interest a charge made for borrowing money

lend to let someone use something you own, which they will give back later

owe to have to pay someone for something they have done for you or sold to you, or to have to give back money that someone has lent you

profit money gained by trade or business

withdraw to take money out of a bank account

Unit 7

ambitious having a strong desire for success, power, wealth, etc.

apply for to request something, especially officially and in writing

assignment a task that someone is given as part of their job

commitment the hard work and loyalty that someone gives to an organisation, activity, etc.

employee someone who is paid to work for someone else

get promoted to be given a better, more responsible job

hire to employ someone for a short time to do a job for you

prospects chances of future success

qualification an examination that you have passed, especially at school or university

recruitment the activity of finding new people to work in a company, join an organisation, etc.

retirement the act of stopping work permanently, usually because of reaching a certain age

staff people who work for an organisation

unemployed not having a job

vocational training training that teaches you the skills you need for a particular job

wages the pay you receive, usually based on the number of hours you have worked

Unit 8

attraction something interesting to see or do

cater for to provide a particular group of people with everything they need or want

display a public performance of something that is intended to entertain people; an attractive arrangement of objects for people to look at

entertainment things to do that interest and amuse people

facilities services or equipment that are provided for a particular purpose

party a group of people that has formed to go somewhere or do something in an organised way

refreshments food and drinks served as a light meal

safari park an enclosed area of land where wild animals are kept, so that people can drive round and look at them

sensational wonderful; very good or exciting

setting a background; set of surroundings

take a break to stop what you are doing in order to rest

take a nap to have a short sleep

take advantage of to make full or good use of something

take pleasure in to enjoy something

venue a place where something such as a concert, performance, etc. is organised to take place

Unit 9

bark to make the short, loud sound that dogs make

bear in mind to remember a useful or important piece of information

breed a type of animal, especially one that people have kept to produce more animals from, such as cats, dogs and farm animals

coat an animal's fur, wool, or hair

encounter to meet someone or something or experience something unexpectedly

erect standing in a straight upright position

groom to take care of animals, especially horses, by cleaning and brushing them

handle to deal with

ingenious very clever and innovative

species a group of animals or plants which are all similar and which can breed together to produce young animals or plants of the same kind as them

stroke to move your hand gently over something

upkeep the cost or process of keeping something in good condition

vaccinate to protect a person or animal from a disease by putting a small amount of a substance containing that disease into their body

virtually almost; very nearly

Unit 10

bring up to educate and care for a child until he/she becomes an adult

cross your mind to come into your mind for a short time

get around to to find time to do something

grow up to develop from being a child to being an adult

keep in touch to stay in contact

kid (informal) a child

only child someone with no brothers or sisters

relative a member of your family

short of not having enough of

solitary done or experienced alone

take after to look or behave like an older relative

upbringing the care, training and education that someone receives when they are growing up

values your ideas about what is important in life; your principles about what is right and wrong

well-off having enough money to live well

Unit 11

budget a plan of how an organisation or individual will spend money that is available for a specific period of time

convict to prove or officially announce that someone is guilty of a crime after a trial

crack down on to become more strict in dealing with a problem and punishing the people involved

culprit the person who is guilty of a crime, or responsible for damage, a problem, etc.

deliberate intended or planned, and not happening accidentally

gang a group of criminals; a group of young people who spend time together and often cause trouble

intruder someone who illegally enters a building or area with the aim of robbing or destroying it

jail term a period of time spent in prison

legislation the act of making laws

maintenance the act of keeping something in good condition

plead to state in a court of law whether or not you are guilty of a crime

probation the system of allowing some criminals not to go to prison, if they behave well and report regularly to a probation officer for a fixed period of time

resident a person who lives in a place, such as a house, hotel or particular area, all the time or just while working, studying or visiting

sentence a punishment that a judge gives to someone who has been declared guilty of a crime

victim someone who has been attacked, robbed, etc.; a person, animal or thing that suffers pain, death, harm, destruction, etc., as a result of other people's actions or a situation

Unit 12

amenities things in a place that make it easier to live there

brochure a thin book, giving information or advertising something

catering the activity of providing food and drinks

comprehensive including all the necessary facts, details or problems that need to be dealt with; thorough

courteous having good manners and respect for other people

delivery the act of bringing goods, letters, etc. to a specific person or place

emergency services the official organisations, e.g. the police, that deal with crime, fires and injuries

fare the price you pay to travel by bus, train, plane, etc.

homeless without a home

inconvenience something that causes you problems or difficulty

leaflet a small piece of printed paper giving information or advertising something

recycling the process of treating things such as paper and glass so that they can be used again

refuse waste material; rubbish

terminal a building where people wait to get onto planes, coaches, etc.; a piece of computer equipment (usually a keyboard and a screen) that you use for putting in or taking out information from a larger computer

transmit to send out electric signals, messages, etc. by radio or other similar equipment

Unit 13

amateur someone who does an activity for pleasure or interest, not as a job

convenient suitable or practical for a particular purpose; not causing difficulty

conventional following what is traditional or is considered to be normal

convert to change or make something change from one form, system or purpose to a different one

filthy extremely dirty

in the pipeline in the process of being prepared or produced

option a choice you can make in a particular situation

pick-up a small open vehicle with low sides, used for carrying goods

reliable that which you can trust; dependable

run out of steam to have no energy left to complete something

smog a mixture of fog and vehicle fumes or other pollutants; a mixture of fog and smoke produced by the burning of coal or other fuels

steep rising or falling quickly at a high angle

track the two metal lines along which a train travels; a path, especially one made by people or animals walking in the same place

trip a journey to a place and back again

unreliable unable to be trusted or depended on

Unit 14

bring about to make something happen

circumstances the conditions that affect a situation, action or event

concrete a building material made by mixing sand, very small stones, cement and water

consequence something that happens as a result of a particular action or set of conditions

conservationist someone who works to protect the environment

deforestation cutting or burning down of all the trees in an area

erosion the process of being gradually destroyed by rain, wind, the sea, etc.

exhaust the pipe on a car or machine which allows gas or steam to escape

hardship difficult conditions

lead-free containing no lead

marine connected with the sea and the creatures that live there

ozone layer a layer of gases that prevents harmful radiation from the sun from reaching the earth

pesticide a chemical substance used to kill insects and small animals that destroy crops

plumage the feathers covering a bird's body

sewage waste material from people's bodies and used water that is carried away from houses by underground pipes

Unit 15

bald having little or no hair on your head

ceremony a formal or traditional set of actions used at an important social or religious event

custom something done by people in a particular society because it is traditional

depict to represent or show something in a drawing or painting

implement a tool or instrument

indigenous (of people, animals or plants) living or growing in the place where they are originally from

myth an ancient story, especially one invented in order to explain natural or historical events

slender thin and graceful

spare additional

tale a story of imaginary events, especially of an exciting kind

trap a piece of equipment for catching animals

tribe a social group consisting of people of the same race who have the same beliefs, customs, language, etc., and usually live in one particular area ruled by a chief

wrinkle a line on your face or skin that you get when you are old

Unit 16

abroad to or in another country or countries

blessed with having something attractive or wonderful

booking a reservation at a hotel or on a plane, ship, or train; the act of making a reservation

break a short holiday

geared to organised in a way that is suitable for a particular purpose or situation

glorious beautiful and impressive

harbour an area of water by a coast which is sheltered from rougher waters so that ships are safe inside it

itinerary a plan or list of the places you will visit on a journey

package tour a completely planned holiday arranged by a company at a fixed price, which includes travel, hotels, meals, etc.

picturesque (about a place) charming and interesting

reputation the opinion people have about a particular person, place or thing because of what has happened in the past

sample to taste food or drink to see what it is like

shore the land along the edge of a large area of water, such as an ocean or lake

sightseeing the act of visiting famous or interesting places, especially as tourists

Unit 17

appliance a piece of electrical equipment, such as a washing machine, used in people's homes

break in to enter a building illegally

commute to regularly travel a long distance to get to work, especially by train or car

cut off difficult to get to and a long way from any other place

domestic concerning the house or home

exterior on the outside or outside surface of something

high-rise describing a very tall building or style of architecture with many levels

insulation the act of covering or protecting a building so that heat, sound, etc. cannot get in or out

man-made produced by people; not natural

outskirts the parts of a town or city that are furthest from the centre

rent the money that someone pays for the use of a room, building, etc. that belongs to someone else

self-contained complete in itself and not needing other things or help from somewhere else to make it work

suburb an area away from the centre of a town or city, where people live

tenant a person who pays rent for the use of a room, building, etc.

Unit 18

automate to change to a system where jobs are done or goods are produced by machines instead of people

breakthrough an important advance or discovery in something you are studying, especially one made after trying for a long time

clone to make an exact copy of a plant or animal by taking a cell from it and developing it artificially

condition to make a person or animal think or behave in a certain way by influencing or training them over a period of time

defect a fault or lack of something that means that something is not perfect

devise to plan or invent a way of doing something

discover to find something that already existed but was not known about

experiment a thorough test using scientific methods to discover how someone or something reacts under certain conditions

immunise to protect someone from a particular illness, especially by putting a substance into their body by injection

inoculate to inject a weak form of a disease into someone or an animal as a protection against the disease

invent to make, design or produce something new for the first time

mass production the making of large numbers of the same article by a fixed method

research (v) to study a subject in detail, especially in order to discover new facts or test new ideas; (n) a serious study of a subject in order to discover new facts or test new ideas

standardise to make all the things of one particular type the same as each other

theory an idea or set of ideas that is intended to explain something about life or the world

Unit 19

attendance being present on a regular basis

bully to hurt or threaten to hurt someone, especially someone who is younger or weaker

curriculum the subjects that are taught by a school, college, etc., or the things that are studied in a particular subject

degree a course of study at a university or college

graduate a person who has completed a university degree course, especially for a first degree

literacy the state of being able to read and write

marginalise to make a group of people unimportant and powerless

motivating making someone keen to do or achieve something

pace the rate or speed at which something happens

pass to succeed in an examination or test

primary (BrE) concerning the education of children between the ages of 5 and 11

secondary (BrE) concerning the education of children between the ages of 11 and 16 or 18

sit an exam to take an examination

term one of the three periods that the school or university year is divided into

truancy the act of purposely staying away from school without permission

tutor someone who teaches one pupil, or a small group, and is paid directly by them

Unit 20

artefact an object such as a tool, weapon, etc. that was made in the past and is historically important

ceramics things that are made of clay and baked until hard

collection a set of similar things that are kept or brought together because they are attractive or interesting

curator someone who is in charge of a museum

exhibition a collection of objects that are shown to the public

gallery a building or room where works of art are shown to the public

hands-on providing practical experience of something by letting people do it themselves

heritage important qualities, customs and traditions that have been in a society for a long time

house (v) to provide space for

ornament an object that you have because it is beautiful rather than useful

priceless so valuable that it is difficult to give a financial value

sculpture solid objects produced out of stone, wood, clay, usually representing people or animals

treasures very valuable objects

EXAM FACTFILE

First Certificate in English
Paper 1: Reading

takes	1 hour 15 minutes
is answered	on a separate answer sheet
includes	• texts of about 350–700 words each • about 1,900–2,300 words overall • 35 questions in total
has texts of these types:	• advertisements • newspaper and magazine articles • fiction • extracts from brochures, guides, manuals, etc. • correspondence, messages • reports
is marked	out of a final total of 40 marks

Paper 1 consists of four parts:

Part	Task focus	Task description	Timing	Questions	Marks
1 Multiple matching	Reading for main points and gist of a text – skimming	You are given a set of prompts (sentences, headlines, titles, etc.) and a text; you must match the prompts to parts in the text. You are given one extra prompt which you do not need to use.	Spend about 17 minutes	6 or 7	Number of questions x 2 marks
2 Multiple choice	Reading for details in a text	You are given a text and a set of multiple choice questions with four options each. You must choose the right option of the four.	Spend about 17 minutes	7 or 8	Number of questions x 2 marks
3 Gapped text	Reading to understand the structure of a text	You are given a text from which some paragraphs or sentences have been removed; you are given the removed parts in jumbled order after the text. You must show where these parts of the text have been removed from. You are given one extra paragraph or sentence which you do not need to use.	Spend about 17 minutes	6 or 7	Number of questions x 2 marks
4 Multiple matching	Reading for specific information – scanning	You are given a set of prompts (usually questions or sentences) and a text which is made up of mini-texts or has several parts; you must match the prompts to the parts of the text.	Spend about 17 minutes	13–15	Number of questions x 1 mark

Candidate Name
If not already printed, write name
in CAPITALS and complete the
Candidate N... ...encil).

Candi...te's sig...ture

Examination...

Centre...

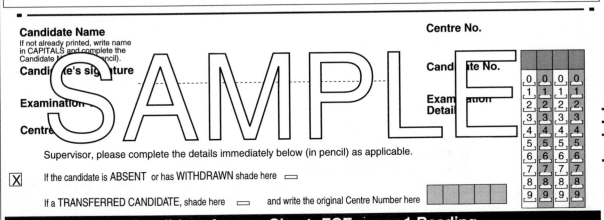

Centre No.

Cand...ite No.

Exam...ation Detail...

Supervisor, please complete the details immediately below (in pencil) as applicable.

X   If the candidate is ABSENT or has WITHDRAWN shade here ▭

If a TRANSFERRED CANDIDATE, shade here ▭   and write the original Centre Number here

Candidate Answer Sheet: FCE paper 1 Reading

Use a pencil

Mark ONE letter for each question.

For example, if you think **B** is the right answer to the question, mark your answer sheet like this:

0   A B C D

Change your answer like this:

0   A B C D

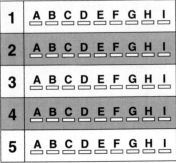

1	A B C D E F G H I
2	A B C D E F G H I
3	A B C D E F G H I
4	A B C D E F G H I
5	A B C D E F G H I

6	A B C D E F G H I
7	A B C D E F G H I
8	A B C D E F G H I
9	A B C D E F G H I
10	A B C D E F G H I
11	A B C D E F G H I
12	A B C D E F G H I
13	A B C D E F G H I
14	A B C D E F G H I
15	A B C D E F G H I
16	A B C D E F G H I
17	A B C D E F G H I
18	A B C D E F G H I
19	A B C D E F G H I
20	A B C D E F G H I

21	A B C D E F G H I
22	A B C D E F G H I
23	A B C D E F G H I
24	A B C D E F G H I
25	A B C D E F G H I
26	A B C D E F G H I
27	A B C D E F G H I
28	A B C D E F G H I
29	A B C D E F G H I
30	A B C D E F G H I
31	A B C D E F G H I
32	A B C D E F G H I
33	A B C D E F G H I
34	A B C D E F G H I
35	A B C D E F G H I

FCE-1

DP318/92

Pearson Education Limited
Edinburgh Gate
Harlow
Essex CM20 2JE
England
and Associated Companies throughout the World
www.longman-elt.com

© Pearson Education Limited 1999

The right of Patrick McGavigan and John Reeves
to be identified as author of this Work has been
asserted by them in accordance with the Copyright,
Designs and Patents Act 1988.

ISBN 0 582 36335 7

First published in 1999

Second impression 2000

Set in 10pt/12.5pt Delta and Wike
Printed in Italy by G. Canale & C

Acknowledgements

Author's Acknowledgements

The authors would like to thank the students at
the Centre for Applied Language Learning in
Illioupolis, and at The Tree Foundation in Voula,
Athens, for their generous time and effort in the
piloting of this book.

The authors would like to acknowledge Amanda
Maris for her patience and editorial skill.

We are grateful to the following for permission to
reproduce copyright material:

Attic Futura for extracts from the articles 'I was
kicked off the team for being a girl' by Claire Baylis
in *SUGAR* Magazine, Sugar/Nike Special,
September, 1996. © Sugar 1996 and 'He's 16,
he's cute and he's won the lottery' by Jo Upcraft
in *SUGAR* Magazine, Issue 35, September 1997.
© Sugar 1997; Andre Deutsch Ltd extracts from *AS
I WALKED OUT ONE MIDSUMMER MORNING* by
Laurie Lee; Conde Nast Publications Inc for an
adapted extract from 'The Making of a Model' by
Charles Gandee in *VOGUE* (American Edition),
August 1994; Andre Deutsch Ltd extracts from *AS
I WALKED OUT ONE MIDSUMMER MORNING* by
Laurie Lee; authors 'agents on behalf of the Gerald
Durrell Estate for extracts from *THREE SINGLES TO
ADVENTURE* by Gerald Durrell, Copyright Gerald
Durrell. reproduced by permission of Curtis Brown
Ltd; Jasmine Moran Children's Museum for an
adapted extract from *JASMINE MORAN
CHILDREN'S MUSEUM* Website; Museum of the
Moving Image for an adapted extract from
MUSEUM OF MOVING IMAGE Leaflet; Random
House UK Ltd on behalf of Mrs Laura Huxley for
extracts from *BRAVE NEW WORLD* by Aldous
Huxley. pubd. Chatto & Windus; Times
Educational Supplement for an extract from
'Tempting Back Absent Friends' by Gerald Haigh
in *TIMES NEWSPAPERS WEB SITE*
www.tes.co.uk 8.4.84.

Photo Acknowledgements

We are grateful to the following for permission to
reproduce copyright photographs:

ACE Photo Agency for page 22 (right); Allsport for
page 4 (top left); Camera Press for pages 42 (upper
middle), 114 (upper middle); Colorific for page 74
(upper right) Greg Evans International for pages 48
(left), 48 (right), 108 (middle), 108 (upper right),
120 (upper right); Eye Ubiquitous for page 82
(lower middle right); Robert Harding for pages 4
(top right), 22 (left), 82 (upper right), 88, 108
(lower left), 114 (upper right); Pearson Education
for pages 42 (left), 120 (lower right); Pictor
International for pages 4 (lower right), 114 (lower
middle); Retna for pages 94 (middle), 94 (right);
Science Photo Library for page 114 (lower right);
The Stock Market for pages 74 (lower right), 82
(lower right), 82 (upper middle left), 82 (upper
middle right), 82 (lower left), 94 (left), 120 (left);
Tony Stone Images for pages 4 (lower left), 22
(middle), 48 (middle), 74 (middle), 82 (upper left),
82 (lower middle left), 108 (upper left), 108 (lower
right), 126 (left), 126 (right); Telegraph Colour
Library for pages 42 (lower middle), 42 (left), 114
(upper left), 114 (lower left); Topham Picturepoint
for page 74 (left)

Illustrations by Kathy Baxendale, Steve Lach,
John Storey and Gecko DTP.

Original cover photo by Jules Selmes
Cover Design by Gecko Ltd
Designed and produced by Gecko Ltd
Project Managed by Amanda Maris